Group's Hands-On™ Bible Curriculum

Grades 3 and 4

Summer

Teachers Guide

JOSEPH

THE TEN COMMANDMENTS

JOSHUA

Group®
Loveland, Colorado

Group's Hands-On™ Bible Curriculum

Group

Hands-On Bible Curriculum™
Grades 3 and 4
Summer

First Printing, 1996 Edition

Credits
Contributing Authors: Liz Shockey, Cheryl Reames, and Jody Brolsma
Editors: Jennifer Root Wilger, Cindy Hansen, and Jan Kershner
Senior Editors: Lois Keffer and Paul Woods
Creative Products Director: Joani Schultz
Copy Editors: Helen Turnbull and Ann Marie Rozum
Art Director: Kathy Benson
Cover Art Director: Liz Howe
Designer: Lisa Chandler
Computer Graphic Artist: Joyce Douglas
Cover Designer: Diana Walters
Cover Photographer: Craig DeMartino
Illustrators: Barbara Coté, Ray Medici, and Steve Zipp
Audio Engineer: Steve Saavedra
Production Manager: Ann Marie Gordon

ISBN 1-55945-592-6
Printed in the United States of America.

CONTENTS

HOW TO USE THIS BOOK

WHY HANDS-ON BIBLE CURRICULUM™?

There's nothing more exciting than helping kids develop a relationship with Jesus Christ. But keeping kids interested in Bible study and Christian growth can be a challenge. Many kids complain that Bible lessons are boring—just more of the same old thing.

We've found a way to get kids excited about studying the Bible. Each quarter of Hands-On Bible Curriculum™ is packed with fresh, creative, *active* programming that will capture kids' interest and keep them coming back for more.

Here's why Hands-On Bible Curriculum will work for you.

A NEW APPROACH TO LEARNING

Research shows that kids remember about 90 percent of what they *do,* but less than 10 percent of what they *hear.* What does this say to us? Simply that kids don't learn by being lectured! They need to be actively involved in lively experiences that bring home the lesson's point.

Group's Hands-On Bible Curriculum uses a unique approach to Christian education called active learning. In each session students participate in a variety of fun and memorable learning experiences that help them understand one important point. As each activity unfolds, kids discover and internalize biblical truths. Because they're *doing* instead of just listening, kids remember what they learn.

Each Hands-On Bible Curriculum lesson for third and fourth grade is based on an important Bible story. Each lesson point distills the Bible story into a simple, memorable Bible truth third- and fourth-graders can apply to their lives.

Your students will be fascinated with the neat gadgets and gizmos packed in the Learning Lab®. And you'll feel good about seeing kids grow spiritually while they're having fun. Keep students interested by revealing the gizmos one by one as the lessons unfold. Be sure to collect the gizmos after each activity so they don't distract students during the discussion that follows. Some Learning Lab items may be used in several lessons, so be sure to hang on to them until this Teachers Guide informs you they are no longer needed.

In each lesson you'll find a photocopiable "Hands-On Fun at Home" handout to send home with kids. Besides providing an important link between home and church, "Hands-On Fun at Home" features great cartoons, family activities, and "Check It Out" Scriptures and questions to get kids and parents talking about the point of the lesson. You can encourage parents' involvement during the next 13 weeks by mailing photocopies of the letter to parents found on page 11.

The items listed below are typical supplies you may use in the lessons in this book. Other items required for teaching are included in the Learning Lab. We recommend that your students use their own Bibles in this course so they can discover for themselves the value and relevance of the Scriptures.

- candles
- cassette player
- chalk and chalkboard
- construction paper
- crayons or markers
- glue or glue sticks
- index cards
- masking tape
- matches
- name tags
- newsprint
- paper clips
- pencils
- plain paper
- plastic trash bags
- scissors
- snacks
- stapler
- thumbtacks
- transparent tape

SUCCESSFUL TEACHING—YOU CAN DO IT!

What does active learning mean to you as a teacher? It takes a lot of pressure off because the spotlight shifts from you to the students. Instead of being the principal player, you become a guide and facilitator—a choreographer of sorts! This doesn't mean that you "check out" of teaching. It's your job to lead students to The Point of the lesson. These ideas will get you started in your new role.

- **Read over your lesson ahead of time.** Hands-On Bible Curriculum lessons are simple to prepare. If you don't want to be tied to your Teachers Guide, consider copying the discussion questions onto a chalkboard or flip chart. Kids can also refer to these written questions to refresh their memories during small group discussions.
- **Be creative in your use of classroom space.** Move your table aside so kids can move around freely and work in groups. Have chairs available but be willing to sit on the floor as well. Chairs can be a distraction, and moving them around slows down your lesson.

● **Think about open areas in the church.** These might be available for activities—the foyer, the front of the sanctuary, a side yard, or a parking lot. Kids love variety; a different setting can bring new life and excitement to your lessons.

● **Get to know the students in your class.** When you meet your students for the first time, call them by name. Find out about their lives away from church. Learn and recognize their strengths. Make affirmation a regular part of your class. Be sure to compliment your students when you see them practicing what they've learned.

● **Be sure to help kids tie each experience to the lesson's point.** The lesson's main point is identified by the pointing finger icon each time it occurs in the text. The Point is worded so kids can easily remember and apply it. Be sure to repeat The Point as it's written each time it appears. You may feel you're being redundant, but you're actually helping kids remember an important Bible truth. Studies show people need to hear new information up to 75 times to learn it. Repetition can be a good thing!

● **Always discuss each activity with your students.** Don't skip over the discussion part of an activity in order to complete additional activities. The activities allow children to *experience* Bible truths. The printed discussion questions and summary statements help students explore their feelings, discover important principles, and decide how to apply these principles to their lives.

● **As you lead discussions with your class, ask open-ended questions.** Rather than rephrasing questions as statements and asking children to agree, wait for kids to answer on their own. Pretend you don't know the answer and let the kids teach you. You'll be surprised how much they know!

● **Encourage kids to explain their answers and learn from each other.** With each discussion question, we've included several possible answers. These answers can help prepare you for responses children might give. You can even use them as prompts if your class has trouble thinking of responses. However, these are not meant to be the "right" answers. Accept any and all answers your kids give.

● **Remember that kids learn in different ways.** Don't shy away from an activity just because you've never done anything like it before. It may be just what's needed to help one of your students get The Point.

● **Make your class a "safe zone" for kids with special needs and learning disabilities.** Avoid calling on students to read or pray aloud if they find it embarrassing.

● **Know your students.** Refresh your memory on what it was like to be a third- or fourth-grader by scanning the chart on page 10. While not exhaustive, this chart will help you know a bit more about the needs, wants, and abilities of the third- and fourth-graders you'll be spending the next 13 weeks with.

● **Capitalize on your students' strengths.** Learn to let your students shine by drawing on their strengths and allowing each of them to make positive contributions to the class. When you're forming groups, include active students with quiet, thoughtful ones. Try pairing children who know the Bible story with children who are hearing it for the first time. Let your students teach each other.

● **If children know a Bible story well, invite them to help you tell it.** Encourage them to share their knowledge with the class, and be ready to fill in if they've forgotten parts of the story.

ATTENTION, PLEASE!

Stand back and get ready for a radical idea: Noise can be a good thing in Sunday school! Educators will tell you that kids process new information best by interacting with one another. Keeping kids quiet and controlled doesn't necessarily mean your class is a success. A better clue might be seeing happy, involved, excited students moving around the classroom, discussing how to apply to their lives the new truths they're learning.

Third- and fourth-graders move fast. If they finish an activity early, you may hear them talking to their friends about school or home life. Or you may see them wrestling or playing together. If you feel as though your room is full of peripheral chatter and motion, don't worry. Kids are used to noisy environments. They're learning a lot in spite of the commotion.

However, you'll need to listen closely for "bad noise"—put-downs, conflicts, and anger. If kids are tormenting or distracting one another during an activity, call for their attention, and explain why the behavior is unacceptable. If you have one or two children who are constantly disruptive, make sure they're not sitting together.

Here are some other tips that will help you keep control.

● **Keep things moving!** Most kids have about a seven-minute attention span—the amount of time between TV commercials. That means you need to be ready to move on to the next activity *before* kids get bored with the current one.

If your kids are too lively to learn during an activity, take a break and use up some energy. Have kids sing an action song, run a relay race, or do some jumping jacks and stretches. Then return to the lesson. You'll find that your students will be able to focus much better. For more ideas, try *Fidget Busters: 101 Quick Attention-Getters for Children's Ministry,* available from Group Publishing, Inc., Box 485, Loveland, CO 80539.

● **Establish attention-getting signals.** Flashing the lights or raising your hand will let kids know it's time to stop what they're doing and look at you. You'll find a suggestion for a classroom signal in the introduction to each four- or five-week module. Rehearse this signal with your students at the beginning of each class so they'll know how to respond. Once your kids become familiar with the signal, regaining their attention will become an automatic classroom ritual.

● **Participate, don't just observe.** Your enthusiasm will draw kids into an activity and help them see you as a friend, not just someone in authority. Get down to kids' eye level so they don't think of you as just another adult, but as an accessible, caring friend.

- **Look for teachable moments.** An activity that seems to be a flop may provide a wonderful opportunity for learning if you ask questions such as "Why didn't this work out?" "How is this like what happens in real life?" and "What can we learn from this experience?" Sometimes children learn even *more* from an activity you felt was a flop!

- **Make the lessons work for your group.** The Teacher Tips in the margins of each lesson suggest ways to adapt the activities for classes of varying sizes. You can use the Bonus Ideas beginning on page 171 to lengthen the lesson. Or use the ideas found in "Remembering the Bible" in the introduction to each module to help kids learn the module's key verse. These fun, active memory-verse activities will help kids remember and apply God's Word in ways that will really make a difference in their lives.

- **If you have a large group or a short class session, pick three or four of the activities you think will work well with your class.** Because you make The Point during each activity, you'll have taught something significant even if you don't get through the whole lesson.

- **If time is running short, finish the current activity and then skip ahead to the closing.** Although kids focus on The Point in each activity, the closing usually includes a prayer and commitment in addition to The Point. The closing activity will reinforce the lesson's point once more and provide a wrap-up for the entire experience.

- **Use the Time Stuffers.** These independent-learning activities will keep kids occupied (and learning!)
  - ✓ when they arrive early,
  - ✓ when an individual or a group finishes an activity before the others, or
  - ✓ when there is extra time after the lesson.

  You'll find a Time Stuffer in the introduction to each module. After a quick setup, kids can use the activity during all the lessons of the four- or five-week module.

- **Rely on the Holy Spirit to help you.** Don't be afraid of kids' questions. Remember, the best answers are those the kids find themselves—not the ones teachers spoon-feed them.

UNDERSTANDING YOUR THIRD- AND FOURTH-GRADERS

PHYSICAL DEVELOPMENT

- Work quickly and with good fine-motor coordination.
- Want frequent repetition of activities they've enjoyed.
- Are interested in active games and organized activities.

EMOTIONAL DEVELOPMENT

- Can have feelings hurt easily.
- Are sensitive to praise and criticism from adults.
- Are developing the ability to empathize with others.

SOCIAL DEVELOPMENT

- Want to be part of a group.
- Enjoy extended group projects.
- Are able to accept limited constructive criticism.
- Naturally avoid interaction with the opposite sex.

MENTAL DEVELOPMENT

- Can read well.
- Like to be challenged but don't like to fail.
- Need to feel independent; don't always want help from teachers.
- Understand cause and effect; like to arrange and organize information.

SPIRITUAL DEVELOPMENT

- Are able to accept that there are some things about God we don't understand.
- Can relate individual Bible events to the scope of Bible history.
- Recognize the difference between right and wrong; are able to make deliberate choices about actions.

Dear Parent,

I'm so glad to be your child's teacher this quarter. With our Hands-On Bible Curriculum™, your child will look at the Bible in a whole new way.

For the next 13 weeks, we'll explore Bible stories and topics to help third- and fourth-graders journey with Joseph, learn about the Ten Commandments, and understand what it means to be true heroes for God. Using active- and interactive-learning methods and a surprising assortment of gadgets and gizmos (such as "prism shapes," a "catch ball ring," and a "wall walker"), we'll help kids discover meaningful applications of God's Word.

Our Hands-On Bible Curriculum welcomes you to play an important part in what your child learns. **Each week kids will receive "Hands-On Fun at Home" handouts to take home and share.** "Hands-On Fun at Home" is a handout containing great cartoons, family activities, and "Check It Out" Scriptures and questions—all focused on the point of our Bible lesson for the week.

Let me encourage you to use the "Hands-On Fun at Home" handout regularly; it's a great tool for reinforcing Bible truths and promoting positive, healthy communication in your family.

Sincerely,

Hands-On FUN AT HOME

JOSEPH

God loved and cared for Joseph throughout the ups and downs of his life. Up: Jacob, Joseph's dad, favored Joseph by giving him a coat of many colors. Down: His jealous brothers sold him into slavery. Up: Potiphar favored Joseph and made him household manager. Down: Potiphar's wife falsely accused Joseph of attempted rape.

Through God's wisdom, Joseph interpreted the king's dreams and eventually was freed from prison and made second in command of all of Egypt. Through God's grace, Joseph and his brothers healed their broken relationship. No matter what happened to Joseph, God used the situation for good.

Like Joseph, third- and fourth-graders experience ups and downs in their lives. They feel the effects of jealousy and competition between siblings and classmates. They feel lonely when parents divorce, undecided about what's right and wrong, and unforgiving when they want to seek revenge. These four lessons about Joseph's life will provide your kids with hope and understanding about a God who loves and cares for them, just as he loved and cared for Joseph.

JOSEPH

LESSON	PAGE	THE POINT	THE BIBLE BASIS
1—JEALOUSY: IT'S THE PITS	17	Jealousy destroys relationships.	Genesis 37:3-36
2—GOD IS WITH YOU!	29	God never leaves us.	Genesis 39:20–40:23
3—WISDOM: GIFT FROM GOD	41	True wisdom comes from God.	Genesis 41:1-57
4—HEAVENLY HEALING	51	God can heal broken relationships.	Genesis 42:1–45:28

THE SIGNAL

LEARNING LAB

During the lessons on Joseph, bring kids back together by sounding one of the *trumpets* found in the Learning Lab. Blow two blasts on one of the *trumpets* whenever you want to get kids back together. In response to the two blasts, kids will immediately stop talking, raise their hands, and focus on you for their next instructions.

Tell kids about this signal—and practice it—before the lesson begins. Explain that it's important to respond to this signal quickly so the class can do as many fun activities as possible. During the lessons, you'll be prompted when to use the signal.

LEARNING LAB

THE TIME STUFFER

This module's Time Stuffer is the "Pharaoh's Palace" poster found in the Learning Lab. Each room on the poster offers Scriptures kids can read and practical ways kids can make God's presence more real in their lives.

During their free moments, kids can go to the poster then look up and read Bible passages about God's presence and love. Then they can sign their names in the rooms containing the ideas they'd like to pursue. The next week, kids can add the dates they accomplished their tasks.

By the end of the month, your class will have learned a lot about God's presence and love in their lives.

REMEMBERING THE BIBLE

Each four- or five-week module focuses on a key Bible verse. The key verse for this module is "But the Lord was with Joseph and showed him kindness" **(Genesis 39:21a).**

Use the following two activities to help your third- and fourth-graders remember this Bible verse and apply it to their lives.

RELAY REMEMBER

Tape two sheets of newsprint to a wall, and place a marker near each sheet. Form two teams and have them line up on the side of the room opposite the newsprint.

Say: **When I say "go," the first team members will run to their teams' newsprint, pick up their markers, and write one way God has shown kindness to them. For example, you could write "good family," "good friends," "nice home," or "God forgives me." Then put down the marker, run back to your team, and tag the next person, who will run to the newsprint and write. Do this until all team members have written on their newsprint. Ready? Go!**

After teams finish, gather kids in a semicircle in front of the newsprint lists. Have a volunteer read aloud **Genesis 39:21a.** Then ask:

- **Was it easy or hard to think of ways that God has been kind to you? Why?** (Easy, because God has given me everything; it was hard to think of something so fast.)
- **What are ways God has been kind to you?** (God gave me my family and friends; God loves and forgives me.)

● **How can you show God's kindness to others?** (Help them; be nice to them; don't talk about people behind their backs; bring them to church.)

Have kids give each other pats on the back for their good teamwork, then repeat the key verse together.

KINDNESS CLIQUES

Gather kids and say: **Walk around the room and say, "kindness, kindness" over and over. When I call out a number, form a group with that number of people in it. Then perform the act of kindness that I will tell you to do. Ready? Go.** Allow kids to walk around the room for a brief time, then say: **Three!**

After kids form groups of three, call out an act of kindness for groups to perform. For example, you could say, "Shake hands," "Scratch a back," or "Smile at each person."

After each act of kindness is performed, have kids mingle and say, "kindness, kindness" until you call out another number and they form new groups with new members.

Depending on the size of your class and the number you call, one or two kids may not have a group. When this happens, have them join you to do the actions.

After kids have performed several acts of kindness, have them sit in a circle. Ask a volunteer to read aloud **Genesis 39:21a.** Then ask:

● **What was it like to show kindness to others?** (I was embarrassed; I liked to be nice; it felt good.)

● **How does God show kindness to you?** (He gave me good friends; God gave me everything; God made a pretty world.)

● **How can you show God's kindness to others this week?** (I can be nice to them; I can smile and be friendly.)

Have the kids repeat the key verse together. Close with a prayer, letting kids each thank God for one kindness he has shown them this week.

LESSON 1

JEALOUSY: IT'S THE PITS

THE POINT

Jealousy destroys relationships.

THE BIBLE BASIS

Genesis 37:3-36. Joseph is sold into slavery.

Joseph's brothers had plenty of reasons to be jealous. Their father, Jacob, loved Joseph more than he loved his other sons because Joseph was born when Jacob was old. Jacob gave Joseph a special coat with long sleeves. In those days, laborers wore shorter garments that freed their arms and legs. The coat upset Joseph's brothers because it signified that Joseph was special and didn't have to do manual labor.

Third- and fourth-graders are not immune to feelings of jealousy. Even in the nicest, calmest child can burn embers of jealousy—when a sister receives a gift from a favorite aunt, when a best friend receives praise from a teacher or coach, or when a parent shows partiality to a younger sibling. Everyone feels jealous at times. This lesson will teach kids about the destructiveness of jealousy and help them replace jealousy with God's forgiveness and love.

Other Scriptures used in this lesson are **1 Corinthians 13:4** and **Proverbs 14:30.**

GETTING THE POINT

Students will

- explore what the Bible says about jealousy,
- discover how jealousy can hurt people and relationships, and
- understand that God can help them handle jealousy.

THIS LESSON AT A GLANCE

Before the lesson, collect the necessary items from the Learning Lab for the activities you plan to use. Refer to the pictures in the margin to see what each item looks like.

SECTION	MINUTES	WHAT STUDENTS WILL DO	LEARNING LAB SUPPLIES	CLASSROOM SUPPLIES
ATTENTION GRABBER	up to 11	**CHOSEN FEW**—Eat a snack and experience jealousy.	Paper balls, Learning Lab box lid	Snacks, plate, sealed container
BIBLE EXPLORATION AND APPLICATION	up to 17	**FROM RICHES TO RAGS**—Act out a modern-day version of Genesis 37:3-36.	Terry ropes, paper balls, prism shapes	Bibles, pair of shoes
	up to 10	**CRACKED UP**—Run a race and discuss what 1 Corinthians 13:4 says about jealousy.	Plastic eggs	Bibles
	up to 12	**GREEN WITH ENVY**—Discuss responses to jealousy-causing situations and read Proverbs 14:30.		Bibles, construction paper, marker, masking tape
CLOSING	up to 10	**BLOW IT AWAY**—Fan away jealousy.	Paper balls, straw fan	Masking tape, construction paper, markers

Remember to make photocopies of the "Hands-On Fun at Home" handout (p. 27) to send home with your kids. The "Fun at Home" handout suggests ways for kids to talk with their families about what they're learning in class and helps them put their faith into action.

THE LESSON

As kids arrive, explain that whenever you blow the *trumpet* twice, they are to stop talking, raise their hands, and focus on you. Explain that it's important to respond to this signal quickly so the class can do as many fun activities as possible. Practice the signal two or three times.

LEARNING LAB

ATTENTION GRABBER

CHOSEN FEW
(up to 11 minutes)

LEARNING LAB

Bring in a snack that can be divided into individual servings such as cookies or graham crackers. Place four servings of the snack on a plate and set the plate on a table. Surround the table with four chairs. Put the remainder of the snack in a sealed container, and place it out of sight. Make sure you have enough snacks to serve all of the students in your class.

Place the *paper balls* in the lid of the Learning Lab box. As you greet your students, ask each of them to pick a *paper ball* from the lid. After everyone has arrived and is holding a *paper ball,* say: **Anyone who picked an orange *paper ball* may go to the table for a special treat. The rest of you must find a seat elsewhere in the room and wait patiently while the others enjoy a snack.**

Collect the *paper balls,* and place them out of sight for use later in this lesson.

After the kids have eaten their snacks, blow the *trumpet* twice, and wait for kids to respond. Have all kids sit in a circle. Ask:

- **What was it like to be chosen to eat the special snack?** (Good, I was hungry; bad, I felt guilty eating in front of everyone else.)
- **How did it feel not to be chosen?** (Bad; frustrated; mad; jealous.)
- **When have you felt jealous in real life? Explain.** (When my sister got a gift and I didn't; when my best friend got a new bike and I didn't.)
- **Was it fair for me to give snacks only to the people who chose orange *paper balls?* Why or why not?** (No, there weren't enough orange balls for everyone; we didn't know which color to choose.)
- **What do you wish would have happened in this activity?** (That I would've been chosen to get snacks; that we all would've been chosen to get snacks.)

Say: **Don't worry. I brought snacks for everybody, and we'll eat them in a moment. If the rest of you never got a snack, you might go on feeling jealous throughout our lesson! Jealousy destroys relationships. Today we're going to learn what jealousy did to**

> **TEACHER TIP**
>
> If you have more than 20 students in your class, give a snack to anyone who didn't receive a *paper ball.* If you have a smaller class, make sure you place at least one *paper ball* of each color in the lid of the Learning Lab box.

> **TEACHER TIP**
>
> This activity will probably cause kids to feel jealous. That's OK. Remember kids' remarks and refer to them later in the lesson.

the POINT

Joseph's relationship with his brothers, as well as what jealousy does to our relationships. But first, let's all eat our snacks.

Bring out the sealed container, and distribute snacks to those students who didn't receive them earlier. Offer seconds to the students who already ate snacks if you have enough. After kids have finished eating, have them help you clean up.

> **TEACHER TIP**
>
> It's important to say The Point just as it's written in each activity. Repeating The Point over and over will help kids remember it and apply it to their lives.

BIBLE EXPLORATION AND APPLICATION

FROM RICHES TO RAGS
(up to 17 minutes)

LEARNING LAB

Blow the *trumpet* twice, and wait for kids to respond. Say: **I'm going to need your help to act out a modern-day version of today's Bible story. We'll all have roles to play in "The Special Shoes."**

Assign the following roles, and distribute the necessary props:

- Jake (the father)—Give him the shoes.
- Joey (the favored son).
- Baby Ben-Ben (the baby of the family)—Give him six *terry ropes* tied together to use as a blanket.
- Brothers and sisters (half of your class)—Give them the *paper balls*.
- Circus people (the other half of your class)—During the skit you'll give them the *prism shapes*.

> **TEACHER TIP**
>
> For the "special shoes" in the story, have the person who plays Joey take off his or her own shoes before the skit and use the shoes as props. Or you could bring a pair of sports shoes from home.

> **TEACHER TIP**
>
> You can assign either boys or girls to play any of the parts. You can assign as few as one or two kids to be brothers and sisters or circus people.

Designate one area of your room as the stage. Have everyone sit behind you, facing the stage. Say: **I'll read a story and cue each of you. When you are cued, step on stage, and do what I tell you to do. And now, ladies and gentlemen, on with the shoe...I mean show... "The Special Shoes"!**

Once upon a time there was a big family. There was the father, Jake. Motion for Jake to step on stage, face the class, and take a bow. **He had many children.** Motion for the children—including Joey and Baby Ben-Ben—to step on stage, face the class, and take a bow. **But of all the kids, Joey was Jake's favorite.** Motion for Joey to take an extra bow.

One day, Jake decided to have a private talk with Joey. Have Jake hook arms with Joey. **The brothers and sisters decided to go play basketball.** Encourage the circus people to step on stage and hold up their arms to form a circle "hoop." Have the brothers and sisters shoot baskets with their *paper balls*. **While the brothers and sisters played basketball, Baby Ben-Ben hugged his blanket and watched the action.** Motion for Baby Ben-Ben to do this. Have the circus people leave the stage. **Meanwhile, Jake decided to give his son Joey a special gift. He bought Joey a new pair of Superstar Sports Shoes.** Have Jake give Joey the pair of shoes. **Joey was so excited.** Encourage Joey to jump up and down, acting happy and excited. **Jake sent Joey to show his new shoes to his brothers and sisters who were all playing**

basketball. Have Jake step offstage and sit by you. Have Joey walk over to his brothers and sisters.

When the brothers and sisters saw Joey coming, they all stopped playing and started to whisper about him. Encourage the brothers and sisters to huddle and whisper. **Joey said, "Hi!"** Pause for Joey to say this. **The brothers and sisters responded, "Hi, hotshot!"** Pause for the brothers and sisters to say this. **Baby Ben-Ben waved.** Motion for Baby Ben-Ben to wave.

Joey showed his brothers and sisters his new shoes. "Hey, look what Dad gave me! Aren't they great?" Encourage Joey to show off his shoes. **The brothers and sisters all grumbled with jealousy.** Encourage the brothers and sisters to grumble. **Joey began to shoot baskets.** Have Joey grab a *paper ball* and shoot a basket.

While Joey was shooting baskets, his brothers and sisters huddled together to think of a way to get rid of him. Have the brothers and sisters huddle and whisper. **Finally, they had an idea. They decided to tie him up and throw him down a sewer.** Motion for the brothers and sisters to stand straight and point to their heads as if they have a great idea. **Baby Ben-Ben had fallen asleep.** Encourage Baby Ben-Ben to sleep and snore. **So they took Baby Ben-Ben's blanket.** Have the brothers and sisters take the *terry ropes,* tie up Joey, then have him sit down to show that he is "down" in the sewer.

All of a sudden, a traveling circus troupe passed by. Have the circus people step on stage. **The brothers and sisters thought of a perfect solution to their problem.** Encourage the brothers and sisters to look at each other and smile. **They could sell Joey to the circus. They could make some money, and they'd be rid of their hotshot brother.** Have the brothers and sisters pull Joey up with the *terry ropes* and hand him over to the circus people. **The circus people paid very well for Joey.** Give the *prism shapes* to the circus people, and have them pay for Joey with the shapes.

Then the circus troupe led Joey away. Motion for the circus people to hold Joey's *terry rope* "leash," step offstage, and sit by you. **The brothers and sisters laughed all the way home when they thought of Joey as a circus clown. They hoped they'd never see him again.** Have the brothers and sisters laugh all the way off the stage and sit down with the rest of the class.

Following the performance, have students bow and clap for each other. Give them one minute to compliment each other on their performances. Encourage sincere compliments such as "Good job of acting jealous, Dave" or "You were a great Baby Ben-Ben."

While kids are complimenting one another, collect the props and place them out of sight for use in future lessons. Then blow the *trumpet* twice and wait for kids to respond.

Make sure all kids are standing, then say: **Raise your hand when you've thought of an answer to each of the questions I'm about to ask. I'd like to hear lots of different, interesting answers. When**

someone gives an answer you've thought of and you don't have anything more to add, you may sit down. When everyone is seated, I'll ask you to stand again for the next question. Ask:

● **How do you think Joey felt when he received the special shoes?** (Good; proud; happy.)

● **How did he probably feel at the end of the story?** (Terrible; sad; scared; lonely; excited to be in the circus.)

● **What caused the bad feelings between Joey and his brothers and sisters?** (Jake shouldn't have given something special to just one kid; the brothers and sisters shouldn't have been so mean to Joey; Joey shouldn't have shown off his shoes.)

Say: **The Bible tells us a story similar to the one we just acted out. The Bible tells us about a favored son named Joseph and his jealous brothers. Let's read the story in the Bible.**

Form pairs. Distribute Bibles and help the students find **Genesis 37:3-17.** Remind them that Genesis is the first book of the Bible. Have kids read the story with their partners. Encourage them to take turns reading the verses. After kids have finished reading the passage, blow the *trumpet* twice, and wait for them to respond.

Then have kids discuss the following questions with their partners. Pause after you ask each question to allow time for discussion.

● **Why were Joseph's brothers jealous?** (Their father liked Joseph better; their dad gave Joseph a special coat.)

● **When have you been jealous of a brother, sister, or friend?** (When my brother got a letter from my grandpa and I didn't; when my friend got a better grade on a test than I did.)

Blow the *trumpet* twice, and wait for kids to respond, then invite them to share the insights they discovered in their discussions.

Have partners take turns reading **Genesis 37:18-36.** After kids have finished reading their passage, blow the *trumpet* twice, and wait for kids to respond.

Then have kids discuss the following questions with their partners. Pause after you ask each question to allow time for discussion.

● **How do you think the brothers felt after Joseph was gone?** (Glad; relieved; guilty; scared to face their father; sorry.)

● **When have you felt sorry about something you'd done because you were jealous?** (I was sorry after I yelled at my brother; I was sorry I ignored my friend.)

● **What are bad ways to handle being jealous?** (Yelling; fighting; not talking to someone; being mean.)

● **What are good ways to handle being jealous?** (Going to my room and thinking about it; praying; talking to my parents.)

Blow the *trumpet* twice to bring everyone together. Wait for kids to respond, then invite them to share the insights they discovered in their discussions.

After kids have shared what they learned from their partners, say: **This part of Joseph's story has a sad ending. Joseph was completely cut**

TEACHER TIP

Encourage active participation in the discussion by following up kids' answers with questions such as "What did you mean by that?" and "Can you tell me more?"

off from his family because of his brothers' jealousy. Jealousy is something that we all feel at times. If we don't keep it under control, jealousy destroys relationships. Let's play a game that helps us see what jealousy can do to our relationships.

the POINT

LEARNING LAB

CRACKED UP
(up to 10 minutes)

Have students count off by twos. Have all the ones form one team and all the twos form the other team. Ask each team to line up single file.

Give each team a *plastic egg*. Have the first two team members in each line hold their team's *plastic egg*.

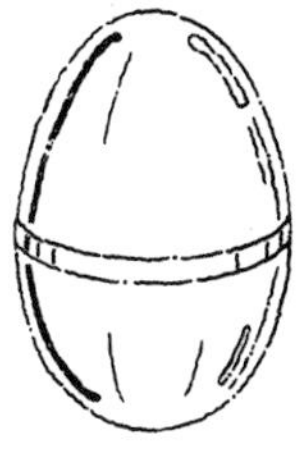

Say: **When I say "go," carry your egg across the room and back again with your partner. If the egg drops or comes apart, you must pick it up or put it back together before continuing. When you get back to your line, pass your egg to the next two people. Keep passing your egg until everyone has had a turn to carry it. The team that finishes first wins! Ready? Go!**

> **TEACHER TIP**
> Make sure there's an even number of students on each team. Participate if necessary to even the sides.

Applaud the winning team. Collect the *plastic eggs,* and place them out of sight for use later in this activity.

Have students sit down in a circle. Then ask:

- **Was it easy or hard to walk across the room while holding the egg with your partner? Explain.** (It was hard because my partner walked too fast; it wasn't hard at all.)
- **What made the eggs come apart?** (Pulling them; going in different directions; they didn't come apart; you had to twist them.)
- **How is the way we handled the eggs in this relay like the way we handle our relationships with people?** (Relationships can break; you have to be careful with people; you have to work together.)

Say: **Relationships are fragile, so we must handle them with love and care—not jealousy. Let's get out our Bibles and read another verse that tells us about jealousy.**

Distribute Bibles and help kids find **1 Corinthians 13:4.** Read the verse aloud together. Ask:

- **What does this verse tell us about love?** (Love is patient and kind; love is not jealous.)
- **What does this verse tell us about jealousy?** (If you are jealous you aren't being loving; jealousy and love don't mix.)
- **The next time you feel jealous, how can you replace that feeling with love?** (Think about something I like about the person; pray; thank God for the person; be nice to the person.)

the POINT

Hold up one of the *plastic eggs,* pull it apart, and say: **Jealousy destroys relationships.** Put the egg back together. **Only God can help us put relationships back together. God helps us get rid of jealous feelings and build loving relationships. Let's talk more about situations that might make us jealous.**

Place the *plastic egg* out of sight for use in later lessons.

GREEN WITH ENVY
(up to 12 minutes)

Before class, make four construction paper signs. The signs should read "Very Jealous," "A Little Jealous," "Not at All Jealous," and "Unsure." Tape the signs to four different walls.

TEACHER TIP

You could use these construction paper colors for your signs: bright or neon green—"Very Jealous," light green—"A Little Jealous," yellow—"Not at All Jealous," white—"Unsure." Talk with kids about what the phrase "green with envy" means.

Gather kids in the center of the room. Point out each sheet of construction paper as you explain this activity to the kids.

Say: **I'm going to read different situations that might cause jealous feelings. After I read a situation, decide how you'd feel in that situation, then go stand under the appropriate sign—either very jealous, a little jealous, not at all jealous, or unsure. When I blow the *trumpet* twice, move back to the center of the room, and I'll read another situation.**

Read each of these situations, and let kids respond by choosing a sign. Have kids form pairs with a person standing close to them under the same sign. Have partners briefly answer these questions after each situation. Ask:

- **Why did you choose this sign?**
- **Has a similar situation happened to you or to someone you know? What happened?**

Blow the *trumpet* twice, then wait for kids to return to the center of the room before you read the next situation.

- **Situation 1—You're in class, and the teacher hands out the test papers you completed the day before. You studied with your best friend all weekend to prepare. Now, when you look at his paper, you see that he got an A, and you received a C-. How do you feel?**
- **Situation 2—The newest, hottest movie is playing at a theater near you. All your friends are going to see it on Friday night. Everyone is going! It's rated PG-13. Your parents say you can't go, but your older brother gets to go. You are . . .**
- **Situation 3—While you're walking around the mall, you see one of your friends buying some new jeans and a jacket. Those clothes cost so much; you know your parents could never afford to buy you stuff like that. Just looking at the jeans makes you feel . . .**
- **Situation 4—Friday night is the birthday of one of your friends. She's planning a big party. You find out that two of your friends have been invited but you haven't. You feel . . .**

After you read the last situation and kids have briefly discussed their choices, blow the *trumpet* twice, then wait for kids to return to the center of the room. Have kids sit in a circle.

the POINT

Say: **We've just discovered some situations that made us feel jealous. Jealousy destroys relationships. Let's discover what else jealousy destroys.**

Distribute Bibles and help kids find **Proverbs 14:30.** Tell kids that Proverbs is in the Old Testament near the middle of the Bible, right after

Psalms. After kids find the verse, ask a volunteer to read it aloud. Ask:

- **What does this verse say will happen if you're jealous?** (You hurt yourself; your bones will rot.)

Say: **Proverbs 14:30 says, "Jealousy will rot your bones." Jealousy destroys relationships, and jealousy can destroy our bodies. This verse tells us that we can be physically hurt if we hold on to a negative emotion like jealousy.** Ask:

the POINT

- **How does your body feel when you're jealous?** (I have a stomachache; I'm nervous; I get a headache.)
- **What do you do when you feel jealous?** (Go to my room; yell; talk to my parents; cry.)
- **How can you get rid of jealous feelings?** (Think about other things; talk to someone; ride my bike; pray and ask God for his help.)

Say: **God understands that we all feel jealous sometimes. Let's see how we can get rid of jealousy with God's help.**

Hands-On FUN AT HOME

We believe that Christian education extends beyond the classroom into the home. Photocopy the "Hands-On Fun at Home" handout (p. 27) for this week, and send it home with your kids. Encourage kids to try several activities and discuss the Bible verses and questions with their parents.

CLOSING

BLOW IT AWAY
(up to 10 minutes)

LEARNING LAB

Have kids help you make a large cross outline on the floor with masking tape. Then form a circle around the cross, and give each student a *paper ball*. If you have more than 20 students in your class, ask some kids to share. Be sure to keep a *paper ball* for yourself.

Say: **These *paper balls* started our discussion about jealous feelings today. In this activity, we'll use the *paper balls* to represent the things that make us feel jealous. Take a moment to think of something that makes you feel really jealous.**

Bring out the *straw fan*, and say: **I'll pass this *straw fan* around the circle. As you hold the fan, say what makes you jealous. Then fan your *paper ball* into the masking-tape cross to remind you that Jesus helps us handle jealousy if we ask him.**

Say one thing that makes you jealous, fan your *paper ball* into the cross, then pass the *straw fan* to the person on your right. Once everyone has fanned away their jealousy, place the *straw fan* and *paper balls* out of sight for use in future lessons.

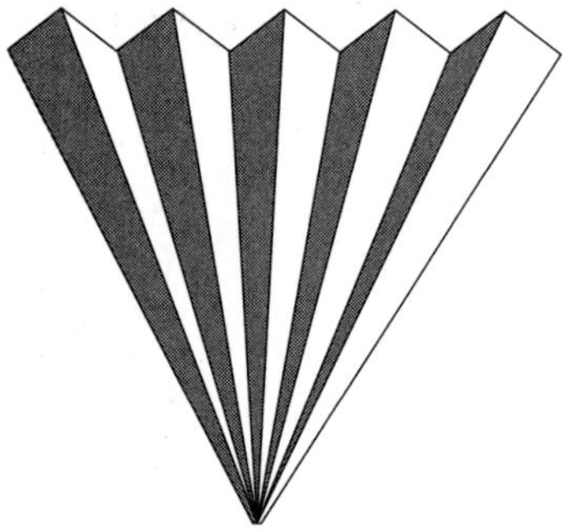

> **TEACHER TIP**
>
> If you have adult volunteers in your class, have them help the kids fold their fans. If not, see which kids catch on quickly to the folding, and have them help others.

the POINT

Say: **You all did a good job of fanning your jealousy away to Jesus. Jesus helps us deal with jealousy. Let's make our own fans to take home so we can remember this lesson on jealousy.**

Give each person a sheet of construction paper and a marker. Say: **Write on your paper one thing you want to remember to do the next time you feel jealous. For example, you could write, "Pray," or "Talk to my parents," or "Thank God for the person rather than be jealous." But don't fold your paper yet.**

Have kids quickly find a partner and share what they've written on their construction paper.

Blow the *trumpet* twice to bring kids together. Wait for kids to respond, then invite them to share insights they discovered in their discussions.

Say: **Partners, help each other fold your paper to make a fan to take home. Fold the paper in 1-inch pleats back and forth, back and forth, so it looks like a fan. Remember the idea you wrote on your fan the next time you feel jealous.**

After the fans are complete, have kids sit in a large circle. Say: **A fan has different uses. We can fan a fire to get it going.** Have kids act like they're fanning a fire in front of them. **Or we can cool things off when we get too hot.** Have kids fan themselves. **Jealousy destroys relationships. When you're feeling jealous, use your fan to cool off, and fan your jealousy away to Jesus. Let's close with a silent prayer. Silently ask God to help you handle your jealousy in the way you wrote on your fan. God helps us handle our jealousy.**

Lead kids in a silent prayer. After one minute, have kids form a group hug as they shout "amen!"

LESSON 2

GOD IS WITH YOU!

THE POINT

God never leaves us.

THE BIBLE BASIS

Genesis 39:20–40:23. Joseph interprets dreams in prison.

Joseph never forgot God's faithfulness. Even in the midst of prison, God was with Joseph, showed him kindness, and caused the prison warden to like him. Because Joseph knew God would never leave him, he continued to do what he had always done: He trusted God, worked hard, and helped anyone he could. When the king's cupbearer and baker were thrown in prison, Joseph helped them and interpreted their dreams. Although the dreams came true, Joseph remained in prison—forgotten by people but still remembered by God.

Third- and fourth-graders feel trapped and lonely sometimes—trapped when they are punished or misunderstood, lonely when their parents divorce or friends fight. Knowing that God never leaves them provides hope for the hard times. This lesson will teach kids that God is always with them and helps them face every situation in life.

Other Scriptures used in this lesson are **Psalm 121** and **Matthew 28:20b.**

GETTING THE POINT

Students will

- discover that God is with them all the time,
- explore what the Bible says about God's faithfulness, and
- learn how they can trust God.

THIS LESSON AT A GLANCE

Before the lesson, collect the necessary items from the Learning Lab for the activities you plan to use. Refer to the pictures in the margin to see what each item looks like.

SECTION	MINUTES	WHAT STUDENTS WILL DO	LEARNING LAB SUPPLIES	CLASSROOM SUPPLIES
ATTENTION GRABBER	up to 10	**DREAM AND TELL**—Create an entire dream by adding on to the beginning of one.		
BIBLE EXPLORATION AND APPLICATION	up to 12	**PATCH TAG**—Play a fast-paced game and read about God's presence in Psalm 121.	Prism shapes	Bibles, masking tape
	up to 20	**RAPPING TOUR**—Walk to four locations and rap the story from Genesis 39:20–40:23.	Cassette: "God-Never-Leaves-Us Rap"	Bibles, cassette player, "God-Never-Leaves-Us Rap" handouts (p. 38)
	up to 12	**PRISONERS AND WARDENS**—Take a blindfolded journey to experience loneliness and read Matthew 28:20b.	Terry ropes	Bibles
CLOSING	up to 6	**CIRCLE SIT**—Form a unique, trusting circle and say ways they'll trust in God.	Learning Lab box lid, prism shapes from Patch Tag activity	

Remember to make photocopies of the "Hands-On Fun at Home" handout (p. 39) to send home with your kids. The "Fun at Home" handout suggests ways for kids to talk with their families about what they're learning in class and helps them put their faith into action.

THE LESSON

LEARNING LAB

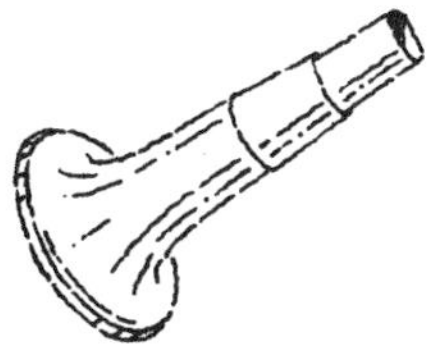

As kids arrive, ask them which "Fun at Home" activities they tried. Ask questions such as "How did your jealousy journal prevent you from being jealous last week?" and "What kind of colored coats or shirts did you make with your family?"

Tell kids that whenever you blow the *trumpet,* they are to stop talking, raise their hands, and focus on you. Explain that it's important to respond to this signal quickly so the class can do as many fun activities as possible.

ATTENTION GRABBER

DREAM AND TELL
(up to 10 minutes)

Have kids sit in a circle. Say: **Today we're going to learn how God helped Joseph interpret dreams. To get started, let's create our own dream. I'll begin by telling a part of a dream. The person on my right will continue when I stop and will add another part. We'll go around the circle until each one of us has added to the dream. You can add something strange, funny, or scary. Use your imagination. Here we go!**

TEACHER TIP
If the students have trouble thinking of something to add to the dream, prompt them with questions such as "What did the kids see or hear?" or "How did they feel and why?"

Begin the dream by saying something like: **One day five kids were walking up a steep, slippery hill. The day was so foggy, they couldn't see very far in any direction. All of a sudden, they heard a sound off to their right. It sounded like...**

Have the person on your right add to the dream when you stop. Go around the circle until everyone has added to the dream. Finish the dream with a happy ending such as: **When the kids finally reached the top of the hill, they found a fast-food restaurant. They could order anything on the menu—free!** Then ask:

- **What do you think was the funniest part of the dream?** (When the kids reached the top of the hill; the ending.)
- **What was the scariest part of the dream?** (When the kids heard the strange noise; not being able to see in the fog.)
- **How do you feel when you wake up from a scary dream?** (Still scared; glad it was a dream.)
- **How do you feel knowing God is with you all the time, even when you wake up from a scary dream?** (Still scared; good; calm.)

TEACHER TIP
It's important to say The Point just as it's written in each activity. Repeating The Point over and over will help kids remember it and apply it to their lives.

Say: **God is always with us. In the daytime or at night, when we're awake or when we're asleep, when we're afraid or feeling alone, God always takes care of us. God never leaves us. In our lesson today, we're going to learn how God helped Joseph interpret dreams. Even though Joseph was in prison, God never left him—just as God never leaves us.**

the POINT

the POINT

BIBLE EXPLORATION AND APPLICATION

PATCH TAG
(up to 12 minutes)

LEARNING LAB

Before the lesson, roll small pieces of masking tape, and stick one to the back of each *prism shape.* Lay the shapes on a table with the tape sides up. You'll also want to clear the room of obstructions for this tag game.

Choose one person to be "It," and give that person one *prism shape.* Say: **This game is played like Tag. When I say "go," It will try to tag you by sticking a *prism shape* patch on your arm and saying, "Remember, God is with you." Once you're "patched," you become It as well. Then both of you run to the table and each pick up another *prism shape* patch. Continue trying to patch others. Each time you patch someone say, "Remember, God is with you." Ready? Go!**

> **TEACHER TIP**
>
> Prepare one *prism shape* for each student in your class. If you have more than 20 students, play the game until all the shapes are used up. Then allow students who are It to continue tagging others by removing their patches and sticking them onto others' arms.

Play the game until everyone has been tagged and reminded of God's presence. Then blow the *trumpet* twice, and wait for kids to respond. Have them sit in a circle on the floor. Ask:

- **What was it like trying to tag someone with a *prism shape* patch?** (Good; it was fun; I got tired of running.)
- **How is this like trying to tell your friends that God is always with them?** (Friends run away and don't listen; I'm too tired to try to tell people; it's fun sometimes.)
- **How did you feel when you were tagged and reminded of God's presence?** (Good; I wanted to be It too; it's nice to know God is with me.)
- **How easy or hard is it for you to remember God is with you every day? Explain.** (Easy, because I remember I heard it at church; hard, I always worry and forget about God.)

the POINT

Say: **No matter where we run or where we play, God never leaves us. He's always with us. Let's read what one Bible writer says about God's presence.**

> **TEACHER TIP**
>
> If kids are playing with the *prism shapes* or using them to create distractions, ask them what it would be like if they focused on God all the time the way they're focusing on their shapes. If the shapes continue to create problems, collect them and put them away.

Distribute Bibles and have students turn to **Psalm 121.** Explain that the book of Psalms is near the middle of the Bible. Have four volunteers each read two verses aloud. Encourage all students to follow along in their Bibles. Ask:

- **What does this Psalm tell you God will do for you?** (Protect me; help me; keep me from danger.)
- **How do you know God is present in your life?** (I see the sun and moon and things God made; my parents love me; my Sunday school teacher reminds me.)

the POINT

Say: **We reminded each other of God's presence when we tagged each other with *prism shape* patches. Although the patch reminders might have fallen off in our game, God never leaves**

us. We know God is present in our lives when we hear friends say nice things about us, when we see the sunshine and stars, and when our parents hug us. Let's find out how God never left Joseph—even when he was in prison.

Make sure students leave the *prism shapes* on throughout the lesson. Encourage kids to think of the *prism shapes* as reminders of God's presence.

RAPPING TOUR
(up to 20 minutes)

LEARNING LAB

Arrange to take your kids to four locations such as these during this activity: the church kitchen, the fellowship hall or an area with comfortable chairs, a basement, and a large storage closet or empty room. The first two locations represent the luxury of Potiphar's house where Joseph was a slave; the second two locations represent the prison where Joseph was sent after being falsely accused.

Say: **We're going to learn a fun and easy rap about Joseph's experience as a slave and as a prisoner. I'll give you a handout with the words so you can rap along with the *cassette tape.* We'll listen to the chorus first, then we'll practice saying it together.**

Give each person a photocopy of the "God-Never-Leaves-Us Rap" handout (p. 38). Play the chorus on the cassette. Encourage kids to join in when the chorus is repeated. Stop the tape after the second chorus.

Say: **Good job learning the rap's chorus! Now all you need is a Bible, and then we'll go on a rapping tour.**

Distribute Bibles and help kids find **Genesis 39.** Say: **Put your handout in your Bible as a bookmark. Bring it along and follow me as we rap around the church together and hear Joseph's story in a new way.**

Lead students to the stations, and follow the instructions on the handout. Take a cassette player along with you for the rapping tour. A portable, battery-powered cassette player works best. Do these steps at each station:

- Have kids sit in a circle.
- Help them find the assigned Bible passage and take turns reading the verses.
- Play the *cassette tape* segment for each station. The *cassette tape* contains each rap verse twice. Have kids listen to the verse first, then rap along with it the second time. After each verse, have kids repeat the chorus with the cassette.

After you've completed the tour, lead kids back to your classroom, and have them sit in a circle. Collect the cassette player and *cassette tape,* and place them out of sight for use in future lessons. Then ask:

- **What did you think about our guided rapping tour?** (It was fun; I learned new things.)
- **What surprised you about Joseph's story?** (I didn't know all that

TEACHER TIP
If you are unable to arrange a tour in your church, simply clear your classroom and travel to the four corners of the room during the tour. Place comfortable beanbag chairs and pillows in two corners to represent the luxury of Potiphar's house; clear the other two corners of any comfortable items to represent the harshness of prison.

TEACHER TIP
Encourage students to provide their own background sounds and rhythm while they rap!

happened to him; I'm surprised he still remembered God with all those bad things happening.)

Say: **We had fun hearing Joseph's story in a new way on our rapping tour. However, this isn't the end of the story. Next week we'll learn how things got better for Joseph because he trusted God. God never left Joseph and God never leaves us. Let's play another game and learn that God is with us even when we feel lonely.**

the POINT

LEARNING LAB

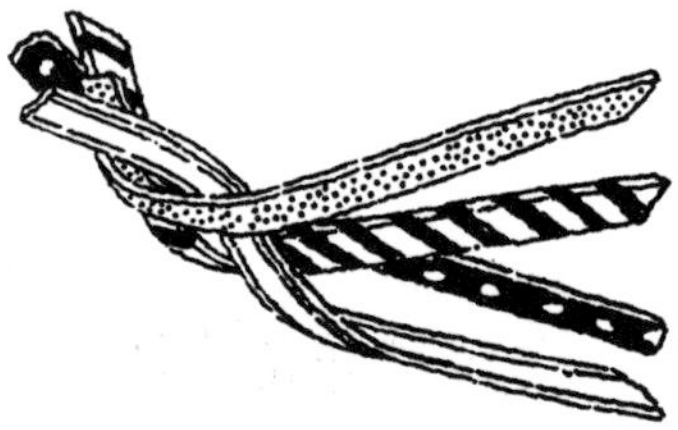

PRISONERS AND WARDENS
(up to 12 minutes)

Gather kids on one side of the room, then have them form pairs. Give one *terry rope* to one partner in each pair.

Say: **Joseph must have felt lonely when he was in prison. But God was with Joseph all the time and comforted him in his loneliness. Let's experience what Joseph must have felt. Imagine that this side of the room where we're standing is the prison cell. The partner holding the *terry rope* is the prisoner. The other partner is the warden. Wardens are in charge of caring for their prisoners. Prisoners, close your eyes so you can be blindfolded with the *terry rope*. During the activity, you must keep your blindfold on—no peeking—and do exactly what I tell you to do. Your wardens will accompany you.**

> **TEACHER TIP**
> If you have more than 12 students in your class, form trios with one prisoner and two wardens.

Have the prisoners close their eyes, then have the wardens carefully tie the *terry ropes* over their eyes. Help the wardens tie the blindfolds if necessary. It's important that students be completely blindfolded for this activity. Encourage the wardens to test blindfolded prisoners' vision before beginning this activity.

Say: **OK, prisoners, your wardens are going to lead you out of your cells so you can get some exercise. You have to be blindfolded because prisoners aren't allowed to see outside of their cells.** Motion for the wardens to lead the prisoners around the room and across to the other side of the room. **Now that you're ready for some exercise, run in place for 15 seconds. Your wardens will hold on to your elbows while you do this. Don't fear, you aren't alone.** Give the prisoners 15 seconds to run in place. Blow the *trumpet* twice to signal that time is up. **Uh-oh, wardens, you forgot your keys back at the jail. Prisoners, stay where you are, and do five jumping jacks while the wardens go back to fetch their keys.** Pause for prisoners to do five jumping jacks and for wardens to walk back across the room. Have the wardens stay there. **Prisoners, your wardens have been called to the head warden's office because they forgot their keys. In the midst of all this commotion, they have forgotten all about you. You have to find your own way back to your cells. Good luck!** Pause while the prisoners walk across the room.

> **TEACHER TIP**
> Have other students help spot the blindfolded kids so they don't run into objects as they try to walk across the room.

Say the following instructions before the prisoners reach their cells: **Wardens, remember your prisoners. Rescue them! Go to them and help them back to their cells!** Pause while they do this.

After the wardens and prisoners reach their cells, have the kids switch roles. Repeat the instructions so all kids experience being wardens and blindfolded prisoners. Once the new prisoners are blindfolded, move to a new spot in the room to repeat the activity. Then have wardens spin the prisoners once before they leave to go find their keys.

After the wardens and prisoners reach their cells, blow the *trumpet* twice, and wait for kids to respond. Collect the *terry ropes* and put them out of sight for use in future lessons.

Have each pair of prisoners and wardens sit together and discuss the following questions. Pause after you ask each question to allow time for discussion. Ask:

- **What was it like to be blindfolded?** (Funny; I could still see; weird; it was dark; I didn't trust my warden.)
- **What did you think when your warden left you?** (I wondered if I could find my way back; I listened to other people's voices; I felt alone.)
- **How was that like being lonely in real life?** (I get scared when I'm alone; I feel like everyone else is having a good time except me.)
- **How did you feel when your wardens rescued you?** (Relieved; better; I knew I could make it back.)
- **How is that like knowing God is with you always?** (It feels good knowing I'm never alone; God helps me when I'm in trouble.)

Blow the *trumpet* twice to bring everyone together. Wait for kids to respond, then invite them to share the insights they gained in their discussions.

> **TEACHER TIP**
> Encourage active participation in the discussion by following up kids' answers with questions such as "What did you mean by that?" and "Can you tell me more?"

After kids have shared what they learned from their partners, say: **When we feel lonely, we need to remember that God never leaves us. Let's read a Bible verse that tells us about God's presence.**

the POINT

Distribute Bibles and help kids find **Matthew 28:20b.** Read it aloud so that students understand where part "b" of the verse is: **"I will be with you always, even until the end of this age."** Then ask students to read the verse aloud with you.

Have kids stand. Say: **Raise your hands when you've thought of an answer to each question. I'd like to hear lots of different, interesting responses. When someone gives an answer you've thought of and you don't have anything more to add, you may sit down. When everyone is seated, I'll ask you to stand again for the next question.** Ask:

- **When are some times that you don't feel as if God is with you?** (When it's dark; when I'm sad; if I'm in trouble.)
- **According to the passage, when is God with you?** (Always; now; forever; until the end of time.)
- **How can you remember that God is always with you?** (Listen to Christian teachers; listen to Christian friends; read the Bible; pray; write

this verse on a piece of paper and put it in my Bible.)

Say: **Jesus promises he'll be with us forever. Our friends may leave us, like the wardens did in the first part of the game. But God never leaves us. Joseph trusted God to be with him at all times. Let's practice some "Joseph-like" trust now.**

the POINT

Hands-On FUN AT HOME

We believe that Christian education extends beyond the classroom into the home. Photocopy the "Hands-On Fun at Home" handout (p. 39) for this week, and send it home with your kids. Encourage kids to try several activities and discuss the Bible verses and questions with their parents.

CLOSING

CIRCLE SIT
(up to 6 minutes)

LEARNING LAB

Have kids stand in a circle then turn and face the back of the person on their right. Have kids scoot toward the center of the circle so they are standing front to back very closely.

Say: **Are you ready to learn some Joseph-like trust? When I say, "One, two, three, trust me!" sit down on the knees of the person behind you. It will work only if you do it at the same time and if you trust the person behind you. When you sit, you'll provide a seat for the person in front of you. Ready? One, two, three, trust me!**

After the first try, blow the *trumpet* twice, and wait for kids to respond. Have kids try it again until they form a trusting, sitting circle.

Once kids are sitting in the circle, say: **Quickly go around and say one thing you trust about the person behind you! For example, you could say, "I trust Sandy will always laugh at my jokes."**

After everyone is affirmed, have kids clap for themselves and the amount of trust they showed each other.

Blow the *trumpet* twice, and wait for kids to respond. Then have them sit on the floor in a circle. Ask:

- **What was it like to trust the person behind you?** (I didn't trust him at first; I was afraid she wouldn't be there; it was fun; I knew he'd catch me.)
- **Do you think these feelings are like Joseph's trust in God? Why or why not?** (No, Joseph trusted God totally; yes, Joseph could've had some doubts; no matter what happened to Joseph, he kept trying and trusting God.)
- **Do you think your feelings in this game are like your trust in**

TEACHER TIP

If your trusting circle collapses, use it as a teachable moment. Ask kids how trusting in people is different from trusting in God. Explore the reasons kids do or don't trust the people in the circle, and encourage them to try again. It really does work if everyone participates!

God? Why or why not? (No, trusting in God is different from trusting in these guys; yes, I know God will be there for me.)

● **How do you know God is with you always?** (The Bible says so; Sunday school teachers tell me; I just know.)

Say: **With a little trust in each other, we formed a sitting circle. With a little trust in God, Joseph was able to interpret dreams in prison. God never left Joseph, and God never leaves us.**

the POINT

Place the lid of the Learning Lab box in the center of the circle, and say: **We've learned a lot today about trusting that God is present in our lives. Think about one thing you want to remember about today's lesson. One at a time, we'll each say what we want to remember, then each of us will take off our *prism shape* and toss it in the lid of the Learning Lab box.**

Start by tossing your *prism shape* into the lid and saying something like: **I'll trust that God never leaves me.**

Once everyone has shared, have kids join hands as you pray: **God, thank you for your promise to always be with us. Help us trust in you as Joseph did. Help us be brave even when things don't go the way we'd like. Thank you for each trusting person in this circle:** (say each student's name). **We love you, God. Thanks for loving us. Thanks for never leaving us. Amen.**

Collect the *prism shapes* for use in future lessons.

TEACHER TIP

If some kids lost their *prism shapes* during the lesson, say: **Even though we lost some *prism shapes* during the lesson, we know we can never lose God's presence. God never leaves us.**

God-Never-Leaves-Us Rap

(Chorus)

God never leaves us. Yes it's true.
He loves me. And he loves you.
Wherever you go, or whatever you do,
God never leaves us. He loves you.

Station One: A Useful Room in Potiphar's House

- Go to the church kitchen.
- Sit in a circle.
- Find **Genesis 39:1-6** in your Bibles, and take turns reading the verses.
- Listen to the first verse once, then rap along with it the second time; join in on the chorus, too.

(Verse One)

Joseph went to Egypt,
became a slave.
At least that deep well
wasn't his grave.
Potiphar bought him,
liked him a lot.
With Joseph in charge
great blessings he got.

(Repeat Chorus)

Station Two: A Comfortable Room in Potiphar's House

- Go to the fellowship hall or an area with comfortable chairs.
- Sit in a circle and make yourselves comfortable.
- Find **Genesis 39:7-20** in your Bibles, and take turns reading the verses.
- Listen to the second verse once, then rap along with it the second time; join in on the chorus, too.

(Verse Two)

With Joseph in his house
Potiphar didn't fear.
To Joseph he entrusted
all things dear.
But Joseph got tossed
into prison to stay
When Potiphar's wife
really lied one day.

(Repeat Chorus)

Station Three: A Scene in the Prison

- Go to the church basement.
- Sit in a circle.
- Find **Genesis 39:21–40:15** in your Bibles, and take turns reading the verses.
- Listen to the third verse once, then rap along with it the second time; join in on the chorus, too.

(Verse Three)

While stuck in jail
Joseph didn't pout.
He did good work,
and the jailer helped out.
He told the cupbearer
what his dream meant.
He hoped from prison
he'd soon be sent.

(Repeat Chorus)

Station Four: Another Prison Scene

- Go to a large storage closet or an empty room.
- Sit in a circle.
- Find **Genesis 40:16-23** in your Bibles, and take turns reading the verses.
- Listen to the fourth verse once, then rap along with it the second time; join in on the chorus, too.

(Verse Four)

The baker was in jail,
and he had a dream too.
When he heard what it meant,
it made him feel blue.
The cupbearer was free,
he went out like a shot.
Did he remember Joseph?
NOT!

(Repeat Chorus)

GO BACK TO YOUR CLASSROOM, AND DISCUSS YOUR TOUR!

LESSON 2:
GOD IS WITH YOU!

the POINT God never leaves us.

Hands-On FUN AT HOME

BIBLE FOCUS

"But the Lord was with Joseph and showed him kindness" (Genesis 39:21a).

SING IT/ Rhyme it

Have a contest! Work as individuals or form teams, and see who can create the best new song or rhyme. Write a song using words such as "God is with us all the time." Sing the words to a familiar tune such as "Mary Had a Little Lamb" or "Twinkle, Twinkle, Little Star." Or write a new rhyme, and say it to the familiar beat of "Humpty Dumpty" or "Jack and Jill." Then sing your new songs, and read your new rhymes. Everybody wins!

FUN food

Prison Toast

With a parent's help, make some prison toast to go with supper one night. Set the oven at 350 degrees. Take several slices of bread (no heels!) and lightly butter both sides. (A sprinkling of garlic salt is optional.) Place a cookie sheet on the lowest oven rack. Place the prepared bread on the rack above the cookie sheet. Bake for 2 minutes or until lines appear on the bread. Turn the bread over and bake for 2 more minutes. The toasted bread will have stripes that look like prison bars on both sides.

CHECK it OUT

Read Psalm 139:7-10.
Give each family member a sheet of paper and a pencil. Have family members rewrite this Psalm for their own lives; for example, "If I go to work, you are there," or "If I go to school, you are there." Read your psalms to each other.

Read 2 Corinthians 11:24-31.
Paul went through a lot of hard times in his life. Tell about a sad or hard time you've experienced. How do you know God was with you and helped you through that time?

MIND boggler

Question: What isn't alive and can't touch you, but can still make you feel scared?

Answer: A bad dream.

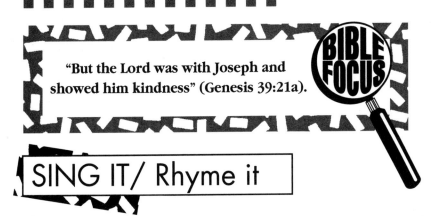

LESSON 3

WISDOM: GIFT FROM GOD

THE POINT

True wisdom comes from God.

THE BIBLE BASIS

Genesis 41:1-57. Joseph rises to power.

When Joseph predicted seven years of famine, people took his prediction seriously. In Old Testament times, annual grain harvests depended on rainfall. In dry years, people from other Middle Eastern regions often went to Egypt to purchase food. People knew they could find food in Egypt because the flooding of the Nile River each year ensured moist, rich ground for growing crops. So famine in Egypt meant disaster. But God was with Joseph and gave him wisdom to predict famine and power to distribute food to an entire nation. God blessed Joseph with amazing discernment.

"Wise beyond their years" may not describe the students in your class, but you can still envision the wisdom that will come with years. Third- and fourth-graders like to feel challenged. They understand cause and effect. They like to arrange and organize information. And they're beginning to feel proud of the knowledge they've attained. This lesson will help kids identify the source of true wisdom and knowledge: God.

Other Scriptures used in this lesson are **Proverbs 3:5-6; James 1:5a;** and **James 3:13-17.**

GETTING THE POINT

Students will
- identify characteristics of wisdom from Scriptures,
- learn that making decisions requires wisdom, and
- discover how to get wisdom from God.

THIS LESSON AT A GLANCE

Before the lesson, collect the necessary items from the Learning Lab for the activities you plan to use. Refer to the pictures in the margin to see what each item looks like.

SECTION	MINUTES	WHAT STUDENTS WILL DO	LEARNING LAB SUPPLIES	CLASSROOM SUPPLIES
ATTENTION GRABBER	up to 10	**MESSAGE IMPOSSIBLE**—Follow instructions to search for a surprise.	Cassette: "Message Impossible"	Treats, cassette player
BIBLE EXPLORATION AND APPLICATION	up to 15	**THREE-PART STORY**—Read Genesis 41:1-57, draw posters, and teach their parts of the story.		Bibles, newsprint, markers, tape
	up to 15	**PARTNER PERFORMANCES**—Practice making wise decisions and discuss what James 3:13-17 says about wisdom.		Bibles, pencils, "What Would You Do?" handout (p. 49), scissors
	up to 10	**WISE-ONE BADGES**—Discuss Proverbs 3:5-6, make badges, and affirm the wisdom of their partners.		Bibles, scissors, markers, construction paper, masking tape
CLOSING	up to 10	**WISDOM TO DECIDE**—Read advice from Scripture stickers and apply the advice to upcoming decisions.	Scripture stickers, cassette: "The Wise Man and the Foolish Man," "Lyrics Poster," Learning Lab box lid	Cassette player

Hands-On FUN AT HOME

Remember to make photocopies of the "Hands-On Fun at Home" handout (p. 50) to send home with your kids. The "Fun at Home" handout suggests ways for kids to talk with their families about what they're learning in class and helps them put their faith into action.

THE LESSON

LEARNING LAB

As kids arrive, ask them which "Fun at Home" activities they tried. Ask questions such as "What psalms and rhyming songs did you write with your family?" and "How could you tell that God was with you last week?"

Tell kids that whenever you blow the *trumpet,* they are to stop talking, raise their hands, and focus on you. Explain that it's important to respond to this signal quickly so the class can do as many fun activities as possible.

ATTENTION GRABBER

MESSAGE IMPOSSIBLE
(up to 10 minutes)

LEARNING LAB

Bring in a special treat that you can easily hide in your pocket or bag such as sugar-free bubble gum or small candies.

Have kids sit in a circle. Say: **Get ready to solve a mystery! Your mission is to find a surprise that is hidden in this room. I'll play some recorded instructions. You follow the instructions, and search the room for the surprise.**

Play the "Message Impossible" segment from the *cassette tape,* and encourage kids to follow the instructions.

When the music stops at the end of the search, stop the *cassette tape.* Have kids sit in a circle.

If anyone asks your advice during the taped instructions, pull that person aside, and show him or her the treat.

If no one asks your advice during the taped instructions, suggest that they ask you for your wisdom and advice now. Show them the hidden treat, then have a volunteer distribute it. Ask:

- **What did you think about the tape's instructions and advice?** (Stupid; not good; they didn't help.)
- **What did you think about my advice?** (Good; you told the truth; you showed us the treat; you should have told us earlier.)
- **How did you finally decide to ask my advice?** (You told us to; we figured you'd know where the treat was hidden.)
- **Who do you ask for advice in real life?** (Parents; friends; teachers; God.)
- **How do you know if a person is wise and will give you good advice?** (Wise people can tell good from bad; they're honest; they're careful; they know what they're talking about.)
- **Why is it sometimes hard to ask for advice when we have a problem?** (We want to solve it on our own; we don't think about it; it's easier to worry than to act.)

Say: **The tape's instructions didn't help you find the treat. Only I**

the POINT

could offer you good advice about where to find it. In real life, true wisdom comes from God. We just have to ask for it. Today we're going to learn that Joseph became a powerful man because he asked God for wisdom.

BIBLE EXPLORATION AND APPLICATION

THREE-PART STORY
(up to 15 minutes)

Before the lesson, write the following three parts of Joseph's story on a sheet of newsprint. Tape the newsprint to a wall.

- Part One: **Genesis 41:1-24**—The King Dreams
- Part Two: **Genesis 41:25-36**—Joseph Interprets
- Part Three: **Genesis 41:37-57**—Joseph Rules

Quickly form three groups, and distribute Bibles. Give each group several markers and a sheet of newsprint. Assign each group one of the parts you have written on newsprint.

Say: **This three-part Bible story tells how God helped Joseph rise to power. In your group, take turns reading your part of the story. Then everyone will be artists and designers. Draw a poster to show what happened in your part of the story. If you don't want to draw pictures, you could write important words or phrases. Choose a "wise teacher" in your group who will present your poster to the rest of the class.**

If groups have trouble thinking of things to draw or write, guide them to the following ideas:

- **Genesis 41:1-24**—Draw the king sleeping with dreams floating above his head. Write words such as "seven ugly cows," "seven beautiful cows," and "Joseph is remembered."
- **Genesis 41:25-36**—Draw Joseph talking to the king. Write words such as "famine," "hunger," and "God helps Joseph."
- **Genesis 41:37-57**—Draw Joseph dressed in fancy clothes as an important ruler. Write words such as "wise," "ruler," and "God gives wisdom and power."

Give the groups about five minutes to read their passages, discuss them, and draw their posters. After five minutes, blow the *trumpet* twice, and wait for kids to respond. Gather the groups, and have a teacher from each group present the group's poster.

Say: **I'll call one group to be first. I'll tape your poster to a wall and have your group's teacher stand by it. All of us will say, "Teacher, teacher, make us wise." Then the teacher will tell the class about your part of the story by describing your poster.**

One at a time, call on the groups to present their posters. Afterward, you will have three posters taped side by side—a complete picture of Joseph's rise to power.

After all groups have shared, ask:

● **How did Joseph grow wise?** (He trusted God; he prayed; he believed.)

● **What good things happened to Joseph because he trusted God and his wisdom?** (God took care of him; Joseph received power; Joseph was respected.)

● **Why is it important for us to seek God's wisdom?** (God knows everything; God knows what's best.)

● **How can you get wisdom from God?** (Pray; read the Bible; listen to what he tells you.)

Say: **Joseph trusted God to help him make decisions. True wisdom comes from God. Sometimes making decisions can be hard. Let's practice making wise decisions.**

> **TEACHER TIP**
>
> It's important to say The Point just as it's written in each activity. Repeating The Point over and over will help kids remember it and apply it to their lives.

the POINT

PARTNER PERFORMANCES
(up to 15 minutes)

Before class, make one photocopy of the "What Would You Do?" handout (p. 49), and cut the cards apart. Form pairs and give each pair a pencil and a card from the handout.

Say: **You'll have five minutes to read your card, decide a wise way to handle the situation, then write your response on your card. Prepare a "partner performance" to show the rest of the class. Decide which part each one of you will play. Then act out how you'd handle the situation. Let's rehearse a performance.**

Read aloud the first situation on the handout, then ask:

● **What wise ways could Partner Two use to respond?** (Say no; invite the person to do something else; pray for God's help in deciding.)

Then say: **For this first situation, Partner Two could pray to God for guidance, then turn to Partner One, and say, "No. I'd better not go to a PG-13 movie. My parents wouldn't want me to. Come to my house, and play basketball instead." Now it's your turn. Those of you who have the first situation, try to come up with a different response from the one we just rehearsed.**

> **TEACHER TIP**
>
> If your class has more than 12 students, make two photocopies of the handout and have more than one pair act out the same situation. Compare their responses.

After five minutes, blow the *trumpet* twice, and wait for kids to respond. Gather kids in a semicircle. One at a time, read aloud a situation, then have the partners stand in front of the semicircle and perform their responses.

After the performances, have kids give one another a standing ovation. Then blow the *trumpet* twice, and wait for kids to respond. Ask:

● **What's hard about making decisions in life?** (Not knowing what to do; not knowing who to ask for advice; making bad choices.)

● **Who can you ask for advice?** (Someone who's wise; someone who's older; someone I trust; I can always ask God.)

Say: **We made good, wise decisions in our partner performances. Now let's see what the Bible says about true wisdom.**

> **TEACHER TIP**
>
> After two partner performances, ask who is remembering to pray and ask God for wisdom before making decisions.

Have kids form pairs with someone other than their "actor" partners. Distribute Bibles and help kids look up **James 3:13-17.** Have partners take turns reading the verses.

After kids have finished reading, blow the *trumpet* twice, and wait for them to respond. Have partners discuss the following questions. Pause after you ask each question to allow time for discussion.

- **What tips did this passage give you about being wise?** (Do good things; be gentle; don't be jealous or selfish; help those who are troubled; be fair and honest; be peaceful.)
- **Which wisdom tip is hardest for you to follow? Why?** (I have a hard time being gentle; I'm not peaceful; sometimes I'm selfish.)
- **Which wisdom tip is easiest for you to follow? Why?** (I'm honest; I can help people who are in trouble; I always try to be fair.)
- **Which tip do you want to follow the next time you have to make a decision?** (I want to be fair; I want to be peaceful and wait for the right answer.)
- **Why is it important to ask God for wisdom?** (God knows everything; God knows what's best; God wants us to do what's right.)

Blow the *trumpet* twice to bring kids together. Wait for kids to respond, then invite them to share the insights they discovered in their discussions.

the POINT ☞

After kids have shared what they learned in their discussions, say: **We need wisdom to make good decisions. ☞ True wisdom comes from God. Let's see what another passage says will happen if we trust God for his wisdom.**

WISE-ONE BADGES
(up to 10 minutes)

Set out scissors, markers, and construction paper.

Have kids stay in their pairs, and assign one partner to be the reader who reads the passage and one partner to be the interpreter who explains what the passage means in his or her own words.

Have kids look up and discuss **Proverbs 3:5-6.** After two minutes, blow the *trumpet* twice. Wait for kids to respond, then ask:

- **What did you learn about wisdom from this passage?** (Trust God; don't depend on your own wisdom; remember God and you will be a success.)

the POINT ☞

Say: ☞ **True wisdom comes from God. Trust him to help you make decisions. Let's remind each other of our wisdom through God by making our partners "wise-one badges." Use the supplies and design a badge any way you want. You could cut out a star shape, a circle, or a square. Complete this sentence on the badge:** "(Partner's name), **you are a wise one because . . . " For example, you could write, "you remember to pray and ask God for advice." We'll exchange badges in five minutes.**

After five minutes, blow the *trumpet* twice, and wait for kids to respond. Have partners stand side by side in a large circle. Give each person a small piece of rolled masking tape to place on the back of each badge.

Say: **One at a time, present the wise-one badge to your partner by reading the compliment, then sticking the badge to his or her collar. Each time someone receives a badge, we'll clap and say, "Way to go, wise one!"**

Go around the circle until everyone has been presented with a badge. Then say: **True wisdom comes from God. We've read about wisdom in the Bible, we've practiced making decisions, and we've made wise-one badges. Let's learn one more wise way to make decisions.**

the POINT

Hands-On FUN AT HOME

We believe that Christian education extends beyond the classroom into the home. Photocopy the "Hands-On Fun at Home" handout (p. 50) for this week, and send it home with your kids. Encourage kids to try several activities and discuss the Bible verses and questions with their parents.

CLOSING

WISDOM TO DECIDE
(up to 10 minutes)

LEARNING LAB

Place the *Scripture stickers* in the Learning Lab lid, and hold the lid. Have everyone sit in a circle. Say: **Think of a decision you have to make this week, something you need God's wisdom for. For example, you may need wisdom to decide what to do with some money you've saved. We'll go around the circle and share our decisions. I'll start first. Once I say my decision, I'll choose a *Scripture sticker* from this lid, then pass the rest of the stickers to my right. When the lid comes to you, share your decision then take a sticker and pass them on. After everyone has a sticker, we'll read the verse together.**

If kids have trouble thinking of decisions, suggest things such as what to do when a friend comes over or whether to join a certain club or team. After everyone has shared a decision, have kids read aloud the verse on their *Scripture stickers:* "But if any of you needs wisdom, you should ask God for it" **(James 1:5a).**

the POINT

Say: **True wisdom comes from God. If we want to be wise in making decisions this week, we have to ask God. Take your stickers home with you to remind you of God's wisdom. Let's close by praying silently, asking God to help us make decisions. Remember, he**

is generous and enjoys giving to us, so he will give us wisdom!

Give kids a minute or two to pray for wisdom. Then close by singing "The Wise Man and the Foolish Man" with the *cassette tape*. The lyrics are printed on a poster found in the Learning Lab.

LESSON 4

HEAVENLY HEALING

THE POINT

God can heal broken relationships.

THE BIBLE BASIS

Genesis 42:1–45:28. Joseph's brothers come to Egypt.

When Joseph's brothers arrived in Egypt to get grain, they didn't recognize Joseph, the food distributor, as their brother. To see if his brothers' attitudes had changed, Joseph put them through a series of trials. They were accused of being spies, sent back and forth from Egypt to Canaan, and trapped by the mysterious appearance of a silver cup in Benjamin's bag of grain. From beginning to end, this passage seems to be building up to Joseph's final revenge. Instead, Joseph revealed himself to his brothers and forgave them. God had healed the brothers' broken relationship.

Third- and fourth-graders may experience the emotional turmoil of broken relationships. Students experience divorce between parents, misunderstandings among friends, and fights with siblings. When they are hurt, kids may be tempted to fight back instead of seeking forgiveness and healing. This lesson gives kids hope and teaches them that God can heal broken relationships.

Other Scriptures used in this lesson are **John 13:34-35** and **Ephesians 4:29-32.**

GETTING THE POINT

Students will

- learn what it means to forgive and be forgiven,
- discover ways to make relationships stronger and better, and
- commit their relationships to God's love and care.

THIS LESSON AT A GLANCE

Before the lesson, collect the necessary items from the Learning Lab for the activities you plan to use. Refer to the pictures in the margin to see what each item looks like.

SECTION	MINUTES	WHAT STUDENTS WILL DO	LEARNING LAB SUPPLIES	CLASSROOM SUPPLIES
ATTENTION GRABBER	up to 10	**PUZZLING**—Draw or write on paper about families, cut up the paper, and discuss broken relationships.		Markers, paper, tape, scissors
BIBLE EXPLORATION AND APPLICATION	up to 15	**BACK AND FORTH**—Act out the Bible story from Genesis 42:1–45:28.		Bibles
	up to 10	**ADVICE LETTERS**—Read situations and write healing advice based on John 13:34-35.		Bibles, pencils, paper, "Advice for Broken Relationships" handout (p. 61)
	up to 15	**TUG O' ROPE**—Play Tug of War two ways, then read Ephesians 4:29-32 and discuss hurtful and helpful words and actions.	Terry ropes, plastic egg	Bibles, tape, newsprint, marker
CLOSING	up to 10	**EGGSTRA-SPECIAL RELATIONSHIPS**—Complete a handout and pray a special way.	Plastic egg	Slips of paper, pencils, "Eggstra-Special Relationships" handouts (p. 62)

Remember to make photocopies of the "Hands-On Fun at Home" handout (p. 63) to send home with your kids. The "Fun at Home" handout suggests ways for kids to talk with their families about what they're learning in class and helps them put their faith into action.

THE LESSON

As kids arrive, ask them which "Fun at Home" activities they tried. Ask questions such as "What wise sayings did your family create?" and "What wise advice did you get from your mom or dad this week?"

Tell kids that whenever you blow the *trumpet,* they are to stop talking, raise their hands, and focus on you. Explain that it's important to respond to this signal quickly so the class can do as many fun activities as possible.

MODULE REVIEW

Use the casual interaction time at the beginning of class to ask kids the following module-review questions.

- **When have you felt jealous in the past few weeks? How did you handle your jealousy?**
- **When was a time God's presence helped ease your loneliness?**
- **What tough decisions have you recently made? How did God give you wisdom to make those decisions?**
- **What's your favorite thing you've learned in the past few weeks? Why?**
- **How is your life different as a result of what we've learned in class?**

ATTENTION GRABBER

PUZZLING
(up to 10 minutes)

Set out markers, paper, tape, and scissors.

Say: **Take a sheet of paper and a marker, and draw a picture of you and your family or you and your friends. If you'd rather not draw a picture, then you may write something about your family or friends. Maybe you can tell about a special day your family celebrated together or a recent vacation. You'll have four minutes to draw or write.**

As kids are working, draw a picture of your own. After four minutes blow the *trumpet* twice, and wait for kids to respond. Show your picture to the rest of the class, then take scissors and cut it into five puzzle-shaped pieces. Ask:

- **What do you think about my cutting up my picture?** (You shouldn't cut up a nice picture; I don't know why you'd want to ruin it.)
- **How would you like it if I were to cut up your picture?** (I wouldn't like it; that would be mean; you shouldn't cut up my property.)
- **What happened to the picture or words on my paper when I**

cut it up? (They were broken apart; parts are missing; they don't go together anymore.)

● **How is that like what happens when you fight with your family or friends?** (Fighting breaks apart my family; I feel like a part of me is missing when my friend is mad at me; I feel hurt and angry when I fight.)

● **How do families and friendships "break apart" today?** (Divorce; fighting; not being nice to each other; death; moving away.)

the POINT ☞

Say: **Families and friendships break apart all the time. In the same way that I cut apart my picture, relationships break apart through fighting and misunderstandings. But ☞ God can heal broken relationships. God can put the pieces back together. Let's experience putting some pieces back together. First you need to cut your own picture into five puzzle-shaped pieces.**

> **TEACHER TIP**
>
> If you have time, have kids glue their pictures to poster board before cutting them up. This will make the puzzles last longer.

Have kids cut their pictures into five pieces. Form pairs then say: **Exchange puzzles with your partner. You'll have 30 seconds to put your partner's puzzle together. When you're both finished, tell your partner about what you drew or wrote on your puzzle.**

After three minutes, blow the *trumpet* twice, and wait for kids to respond. Have kids tape their puzzles back together.

> **TEACHER TIP**
>
> Be sensitive to students who may have experienced divorce in their families. Some third- and fourth-graders may feel guilty and blame themselves when parents divorce. Emphasize to the kids that the divorce is not their fault. Although parents might not get back together again, God can heal the broken feelings that accompany divorce.

Have kids discuss the following questions with their partners. Pause after you ask each question to allow time for discussion.

● **How is cutting up your pictures like breaking a relationship?** (It's hard to handle when it happens; I don't like fights with family or friends; if the damage isn't too bad, you know you can fix it.)

● **What makes a relationship break up?** (Fighting; not listening; getting jealous; saying mean things.)

● **How can you heal broken relationships?** (By saying I'm sorry; asking for forgiveness; being nice.)

● **How is that like taping your picture back together?** (I feel better when it's fixed; it isn't the same as before it was broken.)

● **How do you trust God to heal a broken relationship?** (God says he will help us; God doesn't want us to fight; God wants us to love each other.)

Blow the *trumpet* twice to bring everyone together. Wait for kids to respond, then invite them to share the insights they discovered in their discussions.

the POINT ☞

Say: **Relationships break apart just as easily as our pictures were cut apart with scissors. We could put our pictures and stories back together, but only ☞ God can heal broken relationships. Today we'll find out how God healed Joseph's broken relationship with his brothers.**

Tape the repaired pictures to a wall or tack them to a bulletin board. Make a construction paper sign that says, "God can heal broken relationships." Tape the sign above the pictures as a reminder of this lesson.

BIBLE EXPLORATION AND APPLICATION

BACK AND FORTH
(up to 15 minutes)

Say: **We've seen Joseph go through a lot in the last three weeks. So now we're ready to hear the happy ending to Joseph's story. There's a lot of action in this part of the story, so I'll need your help to tell it.**

Practice the following cues and responses with the kids before telling the story.

- **Whenever I say "Jacob," everyone will raise both arms and say "Daddy!"**
- **Whenever I say "Joseph," the girls will point to their temples and say, "He was wise."**
- **Whenever I say "brothers," the boys will point to themselves and say, "That's us!"**
- **Whenever I say "Canaan," everyone will hop to the right side of the room.**
- **Whenever I say "Egypt," everyone will hop to the left side of the room.**

Read aloud the following story about Joseph and his brothers. Pause after each underlined word to give kids time to do their actions.

The seven years of famine <u>Joseph</u> predicted had arrived. <u>Egypt</u> was the only place that had grain, and <u>Joseph</u> was in charge of the food distribution. In <u>Canaan</u>, <u>Joseph's</u> family was hungry. So <u>Jacob</u> sent the <u>brothers</u> (minus their youngest brother, Benjamin) to <u>Egypt</u> to get grain. <u>Joseph</u> recognized his <u>brothers</u>, but he acted as if he didn't know them.

The <u>brothers</u> didn't know <u>Joseph</u>. And <u>Joseph</u> accused them of being spies. Simeon stayed in prison until the <u>brothers</u> could go back home and return with Benjamin as proof that they weren't spies. So the rest of the <u>brothers</u> took their grain and went back to <u>Canaan</u>. On the way back home, they found some money in their sacks of grain. They didn't know how the money had gotten there, and they were worried someone would think they had stolen it. They arrived back home, and when the grain was all gone, they persuaded <u>Jacob</u> to send Benjamin back with them to <u>Egypt</u>.

From <u>Canaan</u> to <u>Egypt</u> they traveled. When they saw <u>Joseph</u>, the <u>brothers</u> were afraid because of the money they'd found in their sacks. But <u>Joseph</u> took good care of his <u>brothers</u>. He gave them a good meal and a lot more grain to take home. Then <u>Joseph</u> had a servant put a silver cup in Benjamin's sack of grain.

When the <u>brothers</u> started back to <u>Canaan</u>, <u>Joseph</u> sent a guard after them. When the guard looked in the sacks of grain, he found

TEACHER TIP

Have kids help clear the classroom of obstacles so kids can hop from side to side when they hear their cues. You could also do this activity in a fellowship hall, empty meeting room, or outside if the weather is nice.

the silver cup. The guard took the brothers back to Egypt. They thought for sure they were in big trouble. But when they got back, Joseph finally told them who he was. Everybody cried and hugged and celebrated. Then the brothers went back to Canaan to get Jacob. They returned to Egypt to live.

Have kids catch their breath and give themselves a round of applause for their enthusiastic participation in the story. Distribute Bibles then say: **Now let's read about Joseph's reunion with his brothers in the Bible. Read Genesis 45:1-15 with a partner near you. Stand up when you're finished reading.**

When all kids are standing, say: **Raise your hand when you've thought of an answer to each of the questions I'm about to ask. I'd like to hear lots of different, interesting answers. When someone gives an answer you've thought of and you don't have anything more to add, you may sit down. When everyone is seated, I'll ask you to stand again for the next question.** Ask:

- **How easy or hard do you think it was for Joseph to forgive his brothers? Explain.** (Easy, because he loved them and missed them; hard, because of what they did to him.)
- **Why do you think Joseph's brothers were afraid when Joseph revealed who he was?** (They thought he might want revenge; they knew he'd be mad at them.)
- **How do you think Joseph's brothers felt when Joseph forgave them?** (Good; relieved; still guilty.)
- **Which is harder: to forgive someone or to ask for forgiveness? Explain.** (Forgiving someone, because I might still feel mad at them; asking, because it's hard to admit I'm wrong.)
- **How does God help us forgive others?** (If we ask for help, he'll help us; he shows us how to forgive with Jesus; if we pray, we'll get help.)

Say: **Broken relationships heal when people apologize and forgive each other. God is always at work helping us heal broken relationships with families and friends. God can heal broken relationships.**

TEACHER TIP

It's important to say The Point just as it's written in each activity. Repeating The Point over and over will help kids remember it and apply it to their lives.

the POINT

ADVICE LETTERS
(up to 10 minutes)

Form no more than three groups, and distribute Bibles. Give each group a pencil, a sheet of paper, and a situation card from the "Advice for Broken Relationships" handout (p. 61). Have each group choose a reader, a recorder, and a reporter.

Say: **Read your situation, and write a letter advising the people in that situation how they could mend their relationships. Readers, you'll read your group's situation and Bible verse. Recorders, you'll write your group's advice on your sheet of paper. Reporters, you'll read your group's letter to the rest of the class.**

TEACHER TIP

For groups of more than three students, assign encouragers who will urge group members to contribute ideas.

Help kids find **John 13:34-35** in their Bibles. Give the groups five minutes to read their situations and Bible passage, think about their responses, and write letters filled with healing advice.

Offer the groups help as needed. An example of an advice letter for the first situation is: "Dear girls, God wants us to love each other. Love means wanting your friend to be happy. Offer to let your friend buy the dress, or agree with her not to buy it. A dress is not worth your friendship."

After five minutes, blow the *trumpet* twice, and wait for kids to respond. Gather the groups, and have the reporters present their groups' advice letters.

After groups have read their advice letters, ask:

- **What are ways we can fix broken relationships?** (Talk about the problem; help each other out; forgive; say we're sorry.)
- **How can God help us heal broken relationships?** (He forgives us, so we should forgive others; he loves us, so we should love others; God helps us when we ask.)

the POINT

Say: **God can heal broken relationships. God helps us forgive and forget. He helps us love each other. Let's play a game and explore what we can do to get along.**

TUG O' ROPE
(up to 15 minutes)

LEARNING LAB

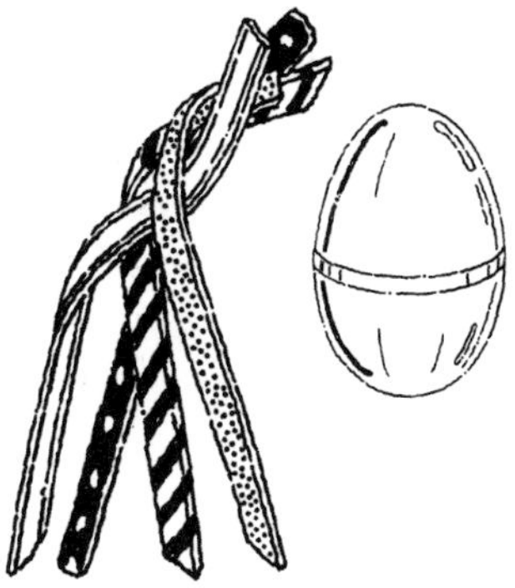

Before the lesson, tape two sheets of newsprint to a wall. Title one "Hurtful Words and Actions"; title the other "Healing Words and Actions."

Form pairs. As much as possible, pair kids according to similar height, weight, or build. Give a *terry rope* to each pair. If you have more than 12 students in your class, form pairs, then position pairs on opposite ends of each *terry rope*.

TEACHER TIP
Be discreet when pairing kids. Third- and fourth-graders are sensitive about their physical appearance.

Say: **We're going to play Tug of War with our *terry ropes*. Before we tug, partners need to stand in the ready position. Each of you hold one end of your *terry rope* and stretch it as far as you can, then stand firm and get ready to pull. On "Ready, set, tug," pull your end of the rope, and try to pull your partner off balance. If your feet move at all, you will be considered off balance. Ready, set, tug!**

Watch while pairs tug. Blow the *trumpet* twice, and wait for kids to respond. Then try the tug again. Blow the *trumpet* twice and wait for kids to respond.

Then say: **Now let's play Tug of War a different way. Partners, get in the ready position again. When I say, "Ready, set, help," do whatever you can to let your partner win. For example, you could simply not pull, or you could say, "You win," and put down your end of the rope. Think of how you can let your partner win. Ready, set, help!**

Watch while pairs do this. Blow the *trumpet* twice, and wait for kids to respond. Then have students sit in a large circle near the two sheets of newsprint you have taped to a wall.

Collect the *terry ropes,* and place them out of sight for use in future lessons. Ask:

● **What was it like to try to pull your partner off balance?** (It was fun because I like to win; she cheated, and it made me mad.)

● **What strategies did you use to get your partner to lose his or her balance?** (I pulled harder than he did; I pulled hard then let up really fast.)

● **How are the things we did in the tug game like things we do to break up relationships?** (We want our own way; we want to win; we want the other person to lose.)

● **What was it like to let your partner win?** (It was weird—I'm not used to playing games that way; it felt good to be nice.)

● **What strategies did you use to let your partner win?** (I just handed him the rope; I didn't tug at all; I talked to her.)

● **How is this like trying to mend a broken relationship?** (We have to be nice; we have to want the other person to win; we think about the other person instead of ourselves.)

● **How can God help us remember to heal rather than tug at our relationships?** (If we pray, he'll remind us; read the Bible; act like Christians; remember Jesus loves us first.)

the POINT ☞

Say: ☞ **God can heal broken relationships. He helps us handle our relationships with gentleness, love, and care. Let's talk about ways to do this.**

Distribute Bibles and help kids find **Ephesians 4:29-32.** Ask four volunteers to read one verse each. Encourage all students to follow along in their Bibles.

Bring out a *plastic egg,* and say: **Let's make lists of things that are hurtful and healing to our relationships. First we'll make our list of hurtful things. Tell me some hurtful things people say or do, and I'll list them on newsprint. Raise your hand if you have an idea. I'll toss this *plastic egg* to you, and you can talk. When you're finished, toss the egg to someone else whose hand is raised. You can talk only when you're holding the egg. When you can't think of any more ideas, toss the egg back to me.**

Allow one or two minutes for kids to toss the egg and tell ideas. List the ideas on newsprint titled "Hurtful Words and Actions."

When kids run out of ideas and you're holding the egg, say: **Now tell me some healing things people say or do, and I'll list them on the other sheet of newsprint. We'll make this list the same way.**

Toss the egg to someone whose hand is raised, then record that person's response on the newsprint. Allow one or two minutes for kids to toss the egg and tell ideas. List the ideas on newsprint titled "Healing Words and Actions."

When kids run out of ideas and you're holding the egg, keep the egg

TEACHER TIP

Encourage kids to get ideas from **Ephesians 4:29-32.** Guide them to think of hurtful things such as "call each other names," "gossip," "yell," and "ignore." Guide them to think of healing things such as "say you're sorry," "help each other," "ask for forgiveness," and "love each other."

for use in the next activity. Then say: **Wow! We've come up with great lists. There are things we can do to hurt relationships. But there are lots of things we can do to heal relationships. God can heal broken relationships. God helps us use healing words and actions rather than hurtful ones. Let's see how.**

the POINT

Hands-On FUN AT HOME

We believe that Christian education extends beyond the classroom into the home. Photocopy the "Hands-On Fun at Home" handout (p. 63) for this week, and send it home with your kids. Encourage kids to try several activities and discuss the Bible verses and questions with their parents.

CLOSING

EGGSTRA-SPECIAL RELATIONSHIPS
(up to 10 minutes)

LEARNING LAB

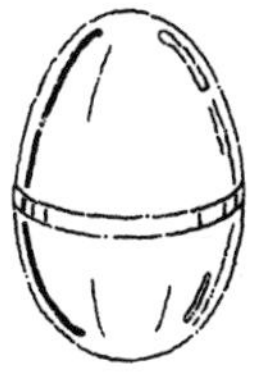

Give each student a pencil and a copy of the "Eggstra-Special Relationships" handout (p. 62).

Say: **First, look at the newsprint titled "Hurtful Words and Actions." Choose one hurtful thing you've said or done recently. Write it on the cracked egg on your handout. Then look at the newsprint titled "Healing Words and Actions." Choose one healing thing you've said or done recently. Write it on the whole egg on your handout.**

After about two minutes, blow the *trumpet* twice to get kids' attention. Say: **Quickly find a partner sitting near you, and share what you've written on your handout.**

After two minutes, blow the *trumpet* twice to get kids' attention. Then say: **Now practice saying kind words to your partner. Affirm your partner for something you appreciate about him or her. For example, you could say, "Deanne, you're always kind to everybody." If you can't think of something, try one of the ideas from our list of healing things to say.**

After two minutes, blow the *trumpet* twice, and wait for kids to respond. Have students sit in a large circle, then ask:

- **What was it like to share healing words with your partner?** (Good; I was embarrassed; I didn't know what to say.)
- **What healing words or actions have you used with friends or family members?** (Saying I'm sorry; praying for others; helping around the house.)
- **How does God help us heal our relationships?** (God wants us to

love each other; God loves us so much he gave us Jesus.)

the POINT ☞

Bring out the *plastic egg,* pull it apart, and say: **We all experience broken relationships, but ☞ God can heal broken relationships. I'll give you a slip of paper. Write down one relationship you'd like God to heal, such as with a friend or family member. After you've finished writing, I'll pass the egg. Put your slip of paper in the egg.**

Distribute slips of paper. Give kids a minute to write on their paper slips. Then collect the slips in the *plastic egg.*

the POINT ☞

Say: ☞ **God can heal broken relationships. He'll help us remember to use healing words and actions with our family and friends. Let's close by offering prayers of thanks to God. I'll start. For example, I might say, "Thanks, God, for your healing love." I'll pass the *plastic egg* to the person on my right who will say "Thanks, God, for..." and add a thought. We'll continue around the circle until everyone has prayed.**

When the egg returns to you, close by praying that God will heal each relationship named on the slips of paper. Encourage kids to take their handouts home to remind them to use healing words and actions. Remove the paper slips, and return the egg to the Learning Lab for use in future lessons.

Advice for Broken Relationships

Situation One

Mary and Sara are best friends. One of their favorite things to do is to go shopping. So one Saturday they went to the local mall. Things were going really well until they both decided they wanted to buy the same dress.

Mary: "I saw this dress first, so it's mine."

Sara: "You did not! I saw it first, so it's mine. How could you have seen it first? You're crazy!"

Mary: "I was here yesterday and tried on this dress. I wanted to come back today so I could buy it."

Sara: "Well, just forget it. If you're gonna be that way, I don't want to be your friend anymore. You can walk home by yourself. I'm leaving."

Read **John 13:34-35,** then write a letter of advice to the girls about how to fix their broken relationship.

Situation Two

Carl and Amy are brother and sister. As usual, they are fighting about whose turn it is to do the laundry.

Carl: "Amy, it's your turn to help with the laundry. I've got to get to a ballgame, and I'm running late already."

Amy: "No, it's not. I did the laundry last time. Mom will be mad if she comes home and finds all this stuff lying around."

Carl: "So do it! I'm sick of you always bugging me. Get off my back."

Amy: "You're the worst, laziest brother I've ever heard of. I'm never going to talk to you again."

Read **John 13:34-35,** then write a letter of advice to Carl and Amy about how to fix their broken relationship.

Situation Three

Sam and Joe have been friends since they were 3 years old. Sam heard that Joe cheated on a test and decides to confront him.

Sam: "Joe, is it true that you cheated on the test today?"

Joe: "No way, Sam. Who told you that?"

Sam: "Kyle said he saw you cheat."

Joe: "Well, I didn't, and if you believe I did, then you're no friend of mine!"

Sam: "Well, if that's how you feel, I guess I'm not your friend."

Joe: "Fine."

Sam: "Fine. I don't want a cheater for a friend anyway."

Read **John 13:34-35,** then write a letter of advice to the guys about how to fix their broken relationship.

EGGSTRA-SPECIAL RELATIONSHIPS

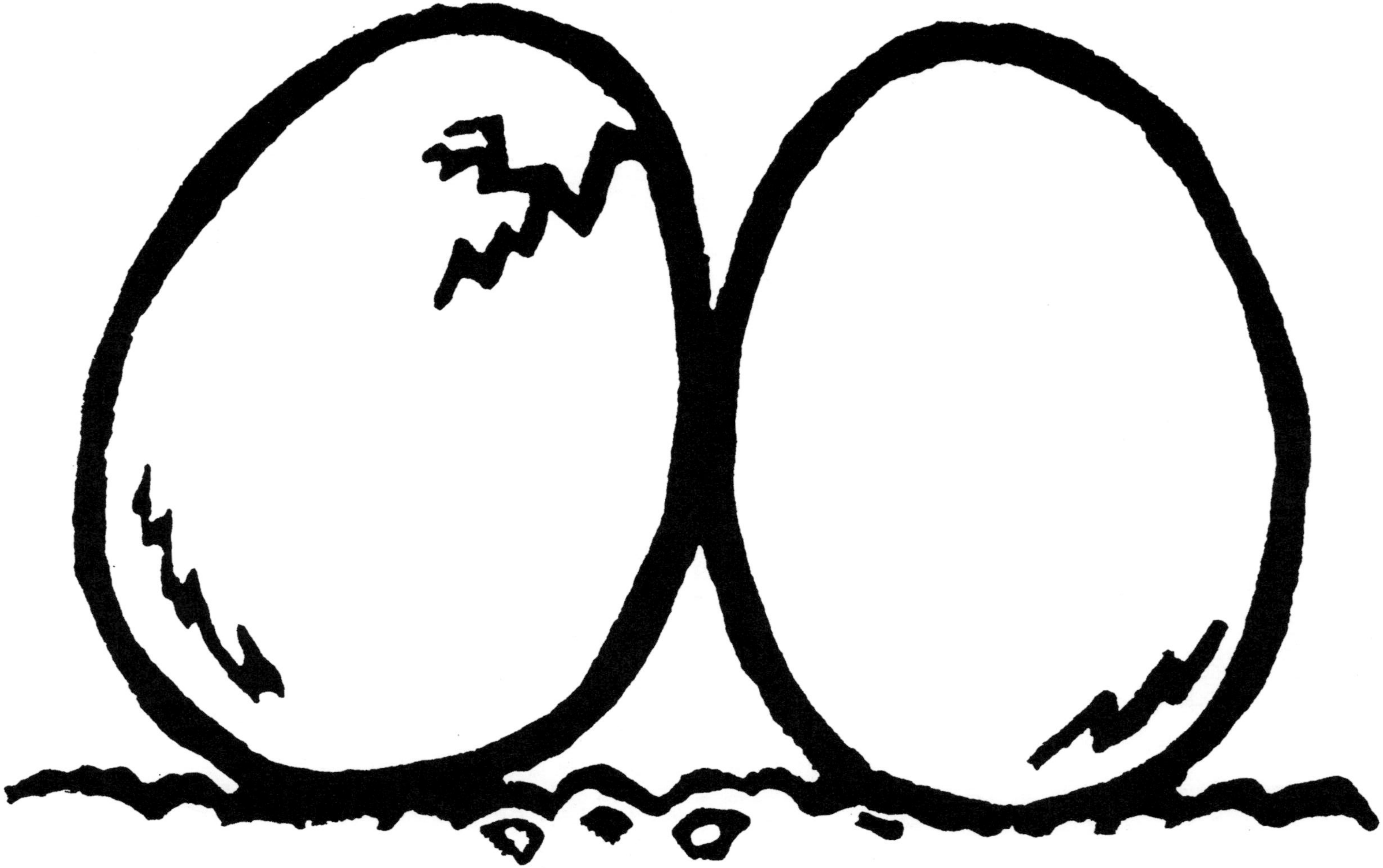

"Do not be bitter or angry or mad. Never shout angrily or say things to hurt others. Never do anything evil. Be kind and loving to each other, and forgive each other just as God forgave you in Christ" (Ephesians 4:31-32).

LESSON 4:
HEAVENLY HEALING

the POINT God can heal broken relationships.

Hands-On FUN AT HOME

BIBLE FOCUS

"But the Lord was with Joseph and showed him kindness" (Genesis 39:21a).

FUN food

Forgiveness Fudge

Here's a simple recipe that works even better when you cook it with a friend. Ask an adult to help you use the stove.

Mix 2 cups sugar and ⅔ cup milk in a medium-sized saucepan. Cook it until a small spoonful of the mixture dropped into cold water forms a little ball.

Then add 1 7-ounce jar marshmallow creme, 1 cup peanut butter (extra-crunchy if you like), and 1 teaspoon vanilla. Pour the mixture into a buttered 9×9-inch pan.

Cool and cut the fudge into small squares. Share the fudge with someone who needs to forgive you or who you need to forgive. It will taste sweeter than if you eat it alone!

NOTABLES

Here's a card to help you and your family members say healing words. Cut out the card and color the letters. Tape the card on your bathroom mirror so that each day everyone in your family remembers to say, "I'm sorry," and "Please forgive me."

Healing words:
"I'm sorry"
and
"Please forgive me."

WAY to PRAY

One night this week, sit down for a family "forgive me" time. Have family members think of one time they might have hurt another family member's feelings. Take turns having each person tell about that time. Don't allow interruptions while each person speaks. The only words allowed after each person speaks are: "I'm sorry. Please forgive me" or "I love you. You're forgiven." Let everyone have a turn to clear the air. Then pray together and have a family hug.

CHECK it OUT

Read Matthew 5:23-24.
Who is someone you need to make peace with? Go to that person, and ask for forgiveness before you go to church next week!

Read Genesis 33:1-5.
Read how Joseph's dad and uncle were reunited. How is this story similar to Joseph's story? How is it different?

THE TEN COMMANDMENTS

What does God want for us? How does God want us to live? What should our relationship be to God and to one another? These are some questions the Ten Commandments answer. The Ten Commandments are rules God gave to Moses on Mt. Sinai for his chosen people—the Israelites. But the Ten Commandments are more than just a set of rules. They're ideals given by God to protect us and help us live lives that are pleasing to him.

Rules! Rules! Rules! Kids love them and hate them. Third- and fourth-graders resent rules that restrict their freedom, limit their pleasures, and prevent them from getting what they want. They love rules that lead to fair treatment, challenges, and rewards. In these five lessons, kids will discover that following God's rules leads to a good life and a fantastic relationship with God.

THE TEN COMMANDMENTS

LESSON	PAGE	THE POINT	THE BIBLE BASIS
5—PUT GOD FIRST!	69	We please God by our worship.	Exodus 20:3-7
6—GOD'S SPECIAL DAY	81	We please God by respecting the Lord's day.	Exodus 20:8-11
7—TOGETHER FOREVER	91	We please God by treating our families right.	Exodus 20:12, 14
8—GOD-PLEASING ACTIONS	101	We please God with our actions.	Exodus 20:13, 15-16
9—DON'T EVEN THINK IT!	111	We please God with our thoughts.	Exodus 20:17

THE SIGNAL

LEARNING LAB

During the lessons on the Ten Commandments, your attention-getting signal will be to sound one of the *trumpets* found in your Learning Lab. Blow the *trumpet* twice whenever you want to get kids back together. In response to the two horn blasts, kids will immediately stop talking, raise their hands, and focus their attention on you. Tell kids about this signal before starting each lesson. Explain that it's important to respond to this signal quickly so the class can do as many fun activities as possible.

During the lessons, you'll be prompted when to use the signal.

LEARNING LAB

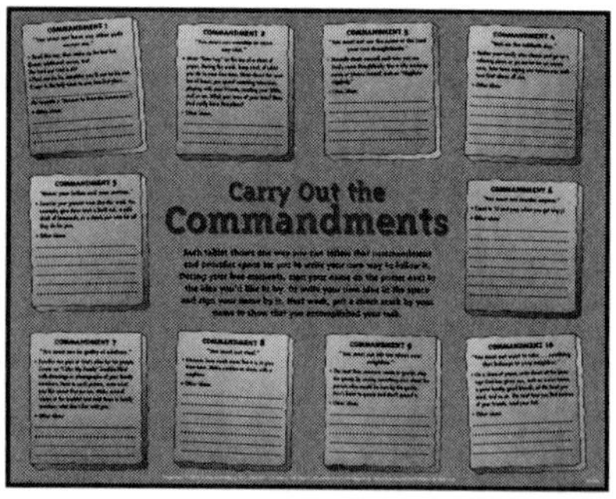

THE TIME STUFFER

This module's Time Stuffer is the "Carry Out the Commandments" poster found in the Learning Lab. Each tablet on the poster shows one commandment and a way kids can follow that commandment. The tablets also contain space for kids to write their own ways to follow the commandments. During their free moments, kids can go to the poster and sign their names next to the ideas they'd like to do. Or they can write their own ideas in the spaces and sign their names by them. The next week, kids can put check marks by their names to indicate they accomplished the tasks.

By the end of the month, your class will have discovered many ways to follow God's commandments.

REMEMBERING THE BIBLE

Each four- or five-week module focuses on a key Bible verse. The key verse for this module is "Love the Lord your God with all your heart, all your soul, and all your strength" **(Deuteronomy 6:5).**

Following are two activities you may do with your third- and fourth-graders to help them remember this Bible verse and apply it to their lives.

LEARNING LAB

ALL YOU'VE GOT

Form pairs. Give each pair a 12-inch piece of *neon kite string.*

Say: **I challenge you to break your piece of *neon kite string* without cutting it. Use all your strength!**

After about two minutes, blow the *trumpet* twice, and wait for kids to respond. Ask:

- **What surprised you about this activity?** (It took a lot of strength to break the string; we couldn't break the string.)
- **How much strength did you and your partner use?** (We used all our strength; not much, we were weak.)
- **What other tasks require you to use all your strength?** (Riding my bike uphill; doing pull-ups in gym class; running a race.)

Say: **The Bible says that there's a time to use all your strength, all your heart, and all your soul.**

Distribute Bibles and help kids find **Deuteronomy 6:5.** Have everyone read it aloud with you. Ask:

- **How can you love God with all your heart, soul, and strength?** (Try hard to do what God wants me to do; read the Bible every day; say my prayers even when I'm too tired; go to church even when I'd rather go fishing.)

Say: **God is the only Lord, and he loves us very much. He wants us to use all our effort and strength to love him back.** Have children repeat the verse with you one more time.

THE ONE AND ONLY!

Tape two sheets of newsprint to a wall, and place a marker under each one. On each sheet of newsprint, draw a big number 1. Form two teams and ask them to line up at the side of the room opposite the newsprint.

Say: **When I say, "Go, number 1," the first person on each team will hop to the newsprint and write the name of something that there's only one of in all the world, such as the Statue of Liberty, Hawaii, or the Eiffel Tower. Then hop back to your line, and tag the next team member, who will repeat the process. Continue until all team members have written on the newsprint. Ready? Go, number 1!**

TEACHER TIP

Accept answers like "Nebraska" or "me." Say: **Although there are other states and other people, each state and each person is unique.**

Applaud both teams for their answers. Have kids sit in a semicircle in front of the newsprint lists. Read the items on both lists to see if both teams agree that only one of each thing on the lists actually exists.

If neither team wrote "God" on its newsprint, write "God" at the top of the newsprint, and discuss how there is only one God.

Distribute Bibles and help kids find **Deuteronomy 6:5.** Have everyone read it aloud with you. Ask:

- **What does it mean to love God with all your heart, soul, and strength?** (I should give God first place in my life; loving God is more important than anything else.)
- **How can you love God this way?** (Give God first place over other activities; try to spend as much time learning about God as I spend learning my favorite hobby.)

Say: **God is the only Lord, and he deserves our love and worship. Remember to use all your effort and strength to love God this week.** Lead kids in saying the verse together.

LESSON 5

PUT GOD FIRST!

THE POINT

We please God by our worship.

THE BIBLE BASIS

Exodus 20:3-7. Honor God's name; worship only God; have no idols.

God made people in his image. That means we are privileged. Of all God's creations, only we were made to worship God. So, of course, God wants to be our top priority. We can worship God through singing, praying, praising, and through our speech and actions. In fact, we can worship God with our whole lives.

Third- and fourth-graders are gaining responsibilities and making more choices about their lives. They are deciding what interests and activities are most important to them. You can encourage the students in your class to make their relationship with God the most important priority. Use this lesson to teach kids to worship God with their whole lives and to give God first place in their lives.

Other Scriptures used in this lesson are **Deuteronomy 6:4-5; Psalm 8:1-9; 16:1-2; 54:2; 116:17; 136:1-3; Matthew 6:9-13; Luke 23:34; Romans 12:1;** and **Hebrews 13:15-16.**

GETTING THE POINT

Students will

- explore what they can do that God's other creations can't do,
- evaluate their priorities,
- discover different ways to worship God, and
- recognize that making God #1 in their lives is a good way to honor God.

THIS LESSON AT A GLANCE

Before the lesson, collect the necessary items from the Learning Lab for the activities you plan to use. Refer to the pictures in the margin to see what each item looks like.

SECTION	MINUTES	WHAT STUDENTS WILL DO	LEARNING LAB SUPPLIES	CLASSROOM SUPPLIES
ATTENTION GRABBER	up to 10	**CREATED SPECIAL**—Think of, then act out gifts that God has given them.	Gift box	Paper, marker
BIBLE EXPLORATION AND APPLICATION	up to 15	**TOPS ON THE CHART**—Rank priorities, place them on a graph, and read Exodus 20:3-7.	Terry ropes	Bibles, index cards, markers, paper
	up to 10	**SACRIFICE OF PRAISE**—Read Psalm 116:17 and other Scriptures and write modern psalms.		Bibles, pencils, "Sacrifice of Praise" handouts (p. 77)
	up to 10	**WAYS TO WORSHIP**—Prepare a prayer, responsive readings, and a song for a closing worship, and read various Scriptures.	Learning Lab, cassette: "How Majestic Is Your Name," "Lyrics Poster"	Bibles, paper, markers, cassette player, "Ways to Worship" handout (p. 78)
CLOSING	up to 15	**GOD IS #1**—Listen to Deuteronomy 6:4-5, and participate in worship and affirmation.	Cassette: "How Majestic Is Your Name," "Lyrics Poster," gift box	Bibles, cassette player

Hands-On FUN AT HOME

Remember to make photocopies of the "Hands-On Fun at Home" handout (p. 79) to send home with your kids. The "Fun at Home" handout suggests ways for kids to talk with their families about what they're learning in class and helps them put their faith into action.

THE LESSON

As kids arrive, ask them which "Fun at Home" activities they tried. Ask questions such as "What did you learn from the Bible passages you read?" and "How did your forgiveness fudge turn out?"

Tell kids that whenever you blow the *trumpet* twice, they are to stop talking, raise their hands, and focus on you. Explain that it's important to respond to this signal quickly so the class can do as many fun activities as possible.

LEARNING LAB

ATTENTION GRABBER

CREATED SPECIAL
(up to 10 minutes)

LEARNING LAB

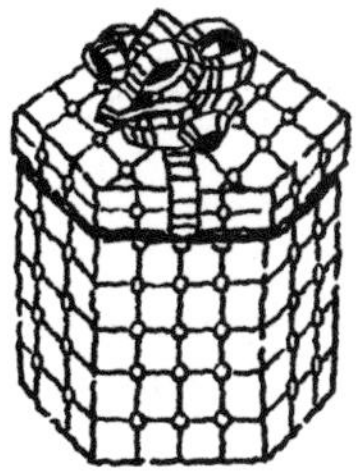

Before the lesson, write on separate slips of paper different examples of God's creations, such as "elephant," "monkey," "cloud," "rock," "watermelon," and "bird." Write one example per slip of paper. Make enough slips so every pair of kids can have one.

Form pairs and give them each a prepared slip of paper. Say: **The name of one of God's creations is written on your slip of paper. God gave each creation different gifts or abilities. Think of something your creation can do that you can't. Then think of something you can do that your creation can't. Finally, decide how to act out what your creation can do and what you can do.**

Demonstrate by saying: **God made the volcano so that it can erupt.** Pantomime with sound effects. **God created me so I can laugh.** Give a belly laugh!

After about two minutes, blow the *trumpet* twice, and wait for kids to respond. Hold up the *gift box,* then say: **This *gift box* represents God's gift to each creation. I'll hand it to one pair, then those partners will act out what their creation can do and what they can do. Then they'll hand the *gift box* to another pair.**

After everyone has shared, gather the slips of paper and the *gift box,* and put them out of sight. You'll need the *gift box* later in the lesson. Ask:

● **What gifts or abilities did God give you that he didn't give to any other creation?** (I can use computers; I can read and write.)

● **How do you feel about God giving you all these unique gifts? Explain.** (Good, I like all the things I can do; bad, I'd rather be a monkey so I could swing through the trees all day; good, I wouldn't like sitting around for hundreds of years like a rock.)

Say: **The most special gift God gave us is the ability to have a relationship with him and to worship him. None of God's other creations can worship as people do. Because God created us in this special way, ☞ we please God by our worship. Let's learn ways we can worship God.**

TEACHER TIP

If you have an uneven number of kids in your class, join the activity and have fun as a participating partner!

☞ the POINT

BIBLE EXPLORATION AND APPLICATION

LEARNING LAB

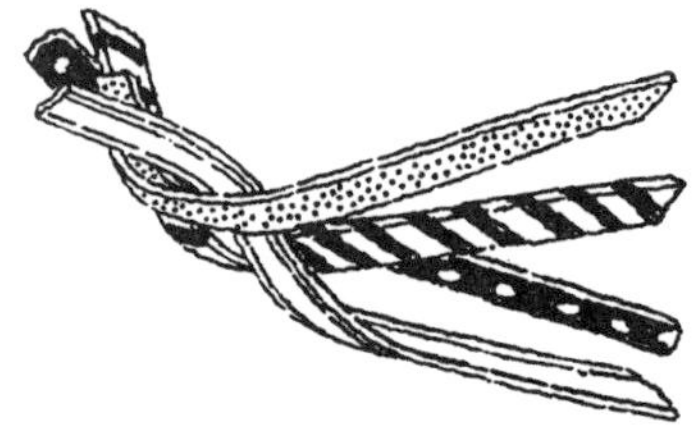

TOPS ON THE CHART
(up to 15 minutes)

Have kids form new pairs. Give each person five index cards and a marker. Say: **Along with our gifts and abilities, God gave us families, friends, and lots of possessions such as homes, games, and bikes. With your partner, help each other brainstorm what kinds of things are important in your life. Then write the five most important things to you, one on each index card. Write large enough so the words can be read at a distance. You'll each need your own set of five most important items.**

While partners are writing, place five *terry ropes* parallel on the floor, about six inches away from each other, to represent lines on a graph. Write "Most Important" on a sheet of paper, and place it next to the top line.

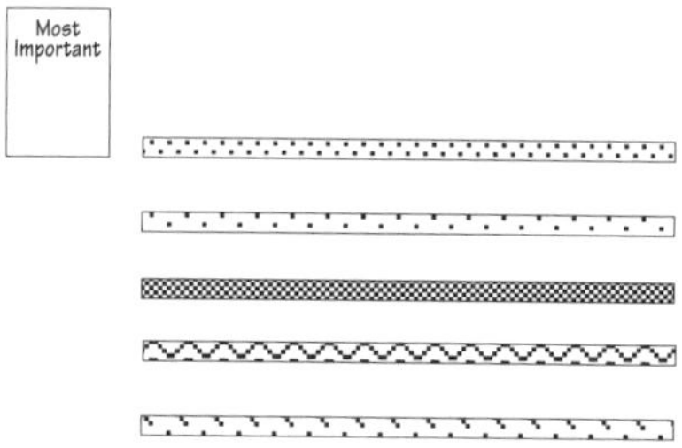

After about three minutes, blow the *trumpet* twice, and wait for kids to respond. Say: **Let's see what's most important in your lives. Read through your cards, and choose one item that's most important to you. Put the card on the top line of this graph.**

Give kids time to choose and place their cards. Say: **Now look at your remaining cards, and choose one that's second most important to you. Place that card on the second line of the graph.**

Continue this process until kids have ranked their five cards and placed them on the corresponding lines. Have kids sit in a circle around the graph. Say: **Let's read the cards and discuss what's most important to us.**

Ask a volunteer to read aloud the cards on the top *terry-rope* line. Then ask another volunteer to read aloud the cards on the second *terry-rope* line. Continue until all the cards have been read. Then have kids stand.

Say: **Raise your hands when you've thought of an answer to each of the questions I'm about to ask you. I'd like to hear lots of different, interesting answers. When someone gives an answer you've thought of and you don't have anything more to add, you may sit down. When everyone is seated, I'll ask you to stand again for the next question.** Ask:

- **What was hard about this activity?** (Deciding what is most important; deciding what is not as important; writing five ideas.)
- **What surprised you about what's most important in our lives?** (Everyone thinks different things are most important; nobody mentioned school; we didn't write some things that should be important to us.)
- **What are some other important things we didn't write on these cards?** (Families; education; God.)

Have kids find their partners from the beginning of this activity.

Distribute Bibles and help kids find **Exodus 20:3-7.** Encourage kids to take turns reading the verses to each other.

After kids have finished reading the passage, have them discuss the following questions. Pause after each question to allow time for discussion. Ask:

- **What do these verses say should be most important in our lives?** (God; obeying God's commandments; worshiping God, not idols.)
- **Why does God command us to worship only him?** (Other things are not good enough to worship; God made us, so he wants us to worship only him.)

Say: **To worship something means to put it first. God wants to be first in our lives. He wants us to worship only him.** Ask:

- **Do you think we tend to worship any items we placed on our graph? Why or why not?** (Yes, if someone took away my Super Nintendo I'd be lost; no, I always place God first.)

Blow the *trumpet* twice, and wait for kids to respond. Invite them to share insights from their discussions.

Write "God" on a sheet of paper in big bright letters. Get out the sixth *terry rope*. Then say: **When we look at our priorities as shown on our graph, have we put God first? Here is where God wants to be.** Place the sixth *terry rope* above the top line of the graph. Place the paper that says "God" next to the new line. Move the sign that says "Most Important" next to it. Ask:

- **What are some ways we can move God to the number 1 spot in our lives?** (Remember that's where God belongs; live our lives as he wants us to; love others because God loves us.)

Say: **We honor God by giving God top priority in our lives. Giving God an important place in our lives is a way to worship. We please God by our worship.**

Gather the *terry ropes*, signs, and index cards, and put them out of sight. You'll use the *terry ropes* in future lessons.

> **TEACHER TIP**
>
> It's important to say The Point just as it's written in each activity. Repeating The Point over and over will help kids remember it and apply it to their lives.

the POINT

SACRIFICE OF PRAISE
(up to 10 minutes)

Say: **God's command to worship only him is so important that it's the very first of the Ten Commandments. We can worship God in many ways.** Ask:

- **How do we worship God?** (By praying; singing; reading the Bible.)

Say: **Another way we can worship God is through offerings. When we give an offering to God, we're giving him back part of what he's given us. Because God has given us so many good things, we want to give him things that are good or important.** Ask:

- **What things are important to you?** (My bike; my Super Nintendo; my family.)

Say: **When we give up something that's important to us, we call**

that a sacrifice. Because the Israelites often earned their living by farming, crops and herds of animals were important to them. They brought grain or animals to give back to God as sacrifices. Let's read a Bible verse to help us discover what kind of sacrifice we can give to God.

Help kids find **Romans 12:1.** Have a volunteer read the verse aloud while others follow along in their Bibles. Ask:

- **What does this verse say about sacrifice?** (Our lives are a sacrifice; our offering should please God; our offering should be only for God.)
- **How can our lives be a sacrifice?** (When we live like God wants us to; when we help others; when we love and forgive others.)

Say: **Let's read what another passage says about sacrifice as a way to worship.**

Help kids find **Hebrews 13:15-16.** Have a volunteer read the passage aloud while others follow along in their Bibles. Ask:

- **What does this passage say about sacrifice?** (It's praising God; it's doing good for others; it's sharing with others.)

Say: **Although we don't bring grain or animal offerings like the Israelites did, we can offer our lives as a sacrifice to God. We can praise and thank God. We can help others in need.**

Form pairs. Give each person a pencil and a "Sacrifice of Praise" handout (p. 77). Say: **Let's make our own "sacrifices of praise" now. Read the verse on your handout, then work with your partner to write your own psalms of praise to God by completing the sentences. After a few minutes, we'll read our psalms.**

After about four minutes, blow the *trumpet* twice, and wait for kids to respond. Have kids sit in a circle, then have them take turns reading their psalms.

Say: **Good job, psalm writers! We can offer our lives as special sacrifices to God through how we live, how we give thanks, and how we do good for others. We please God by our worship.**

TEACHER TIP

Encourage active participation by following up kids' responses with questions such as "What did you mean by that?" and "Can you tell me more?"

the POINT

LEARNING LAB

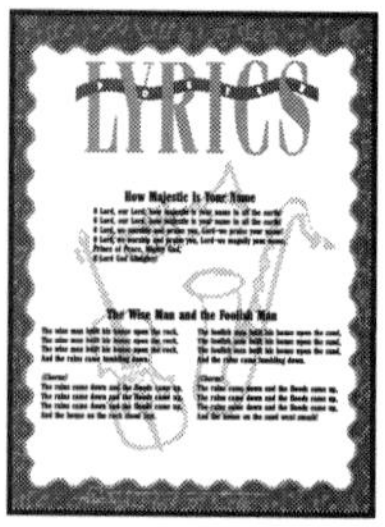

WAYS TO WORSHIP
(up to 10 minutes)

Before class, set up the following three worship centers in separate corners of your room.

- Worship center 1: Set out the Learning Lab, Bibles, paper, and markers.
- Worship center 2: Set out Bibles, paper, and markers.
- Worship center 3: Set out Bibles, a cassette player, the *cassette tape* cued to the song "How Majestic Is Your Name," and the "Lyrics Poster" from the Learning Lab.

Say: **We honor and worship God in many ways. We've talked about making God number 1 in our lives, and we've talked about sacrifices or offerings. Let's learn more about some other ways to worship.**

Form three groups. Give each group a card from the "Ways to

Worship" handout (p. 78), and have each group go to the corresponding corner of the room.

Say: **I've set out supplies in three corners of our room so each group can prepare a portion of a mini–worship service. Read your card, then follow the instructions to prepare your portion of the worship.**

After five minutes, blow the *trumpet* twice, and wait for kids to respond.

Say: **We please God by our worship. Let's worship God by doing what you prepared in your worship centers.**

TEACHER TIP

Circulate among the three groups, offering help where needed.

the POINT

Hands-On FUN AT HOME

We believe that Christian education extends beyond the classroom into the home. Photocopy the "Hands-On Fun at Home" handout (p. 79) for this week, and send it home with your kids. Encourage kids to try several activities and discuss the Bible verses and questions with their parents.

CLOSING

GOD IS #1
(up to 15 minutes)

LEARNING LAB

Gather the entire class in worship center 1 for prayer. Say: **We'll begin our worship with prayer. Then we'll go to the other two worship centers. When we're in your group's center, tell us about your way to worship, then lead us in what you've prepared.**

Proceed from center to center—first for prayer, then responsive reading, and finally for singing. Finish the worship service by reading aloud **Deuteronomy 6:4-5** as a closing prayer. Have kids shout "amen!"

Then form a large circle in the center of the room. Hold the *gift box.*

the POINT

Say: **A special gift God has given to us is the ability to worship and honor him. We please God by our worship. God has given us the Ten Commandments to help us know how to honor and worship him. Today we learned two commandments that teach us to put God first in our lives. Let's close by thinking of ways we can put God first. As you receive the *gift box,* say, "I'm God's special creation. I can put God first in my life by..." and then say your idea. For example, you could complete the sentence by saying, "...by loving others," or "...by praising him," or "...by praying to him." If someone says what you wanted to say, that's OK. You can say it, too.**

Start by saying something like "I'm God's special creation. I can put God first in my life by thanking him in all situations." Pass the *gift box* to the person on your right. Continue around the circle until everyone has had a turn to complete the sentence.

Close with a prayer asking for God's help in putting him first in life. Collect the *gift box, cassette tape,* poster, and other Learning Lab items for use in future lessons.

Sacrifice of Praise

Many of the psalms in the Bible were written as prayers. Read Psalm 116:17, then offer your own prayer of thanks to God by completing these sentences.

I want to worship you, Lord, because . . .

Lord, I thank you for . . .

I will praise you because . . .

Ways to Worship

WORSHIP CENTER 1

Prayers

Praying is one way to worship God. Praying means talking to God. When Christians worship together, they may say prayers out loud or silently. At other times, one person may say or read a prayer. When people pray, they may praise and thank God or ask God for help and forgiveness.

1. Read some of these prayers from the Bible: Psalm 16:1-2; 54:2; Matthew 6:9-13; and Luke 23:34.

2. Write a prayer to use for our closing worship. Here are some ideas:

- Take the *gift box* from the Learning Lab. Hold it above a person's head, and have everyone take turns completing this affirmation prayer: "Thank you, God, for (name), because . . ." For example, you could say, "because of his smiles during class" or "because of her friendliness." Affirm each student in the class this way.
- Write your own prayer on a sheet of paper. Write in large letters so everyone can read along with you. Have the class shout "amen!"
- Set out the Learning Lab. Use each Learning Lab item in a prayer. For example:

Prism shapes—Hold the shapes up, and let them fall to the ground. Pray, "Thanks for your sparkling gift of forgiveness."

Miniature trophy—Hold the trophy up, and pray, "Thanks for making us #1 children of God."

Straw fan—Fan yourself, and pray, "Thanks for your cooling love when we feel angry."

Catch ball ring—Wear the ring, toss the ball, and try to catch it on the ring. Pray, "No matter how hard we try, we can't earn your love. Thanks for the free gift."

Terry rope—Tie it in a bow, and pray, "Help us remember to love others as you love us."

Miniature tool kit—Hold up each tool, and pantomime using it. Pray, "Help us show your love by helping needy or lonely people in our lives."

WORSHIP CENTER 2

Responsive Readings

Responsive readings are a way to worship God. One person or group says part of a prayer or psalm, and another person or group says the next part. Responsive readings give everyone a chance to participate in worshiping God.

1. Read Psalm 136:1-3.

2. Lead a responsive reading for our closing worship. Decide how to read Psalm 136:1-3 responsively. Practice reading the passage then leading it. Here are some ideas:

- Your group could read the first sentence. The rest of the class could read the second sentence. Your group could read the third, and so on, until the entire passage is read.
- Your group could read a sentence, and the class could respond, "We love you and worship you, God!" Your group could continue in this manner, reading each sentence and pausing for the class to respond.
- Lead motions to go with the sentences. For example:

"Give thanks to the Lord because he is good." *(Hold both hands up and look to heaven.)*

"His love continues forever." *(Hold both hands over your heart.)*

"Give thanks to the God of gods." *(Hold both hands up and look to heaven.)*

"His love continues forever." *(Hug yourself.)*

"Give thanks to the Lord of lords." *(Hold both hands up and look to heaven.)*

"His love continues forever." *(Give a thumbs up sign.)*

WORSHIP CENTER 3

Singing

Singing songs is a way to worship God. Some worship songs are called hymns. There are all kinds of praise and thanksgiving hymns. The Bible contains many songs. Some psalms are hymns that people sing to worship God.

1. Read Psalm 8:1-9. The person who wrote the song "How Majestic Is Your Name" used words from Psalm 8:1 and 9.

2. Listen to the song "How Majestic Is Your Name" on the *cassette tape*. Then prepare to teach the song to the whole class for our closing worship. Here are some ideas:

- Play the song once so everyone can hear it. Have one person hold up the "Lyrics Poster" so people can read the lyrics, another person push the play button on the cassette player, and another person be the choir director.
- Rewind the tape and play it again. Have everyone sing.
- Play the song one more time, and have everyone clap to the beat!

LESSON 5:
PUT GOD FIRST!

the POINT **We please God by our worship.**

Hands-On FUN AT HOME

BIBLE FOCUS

"Love the Lord your God with all your heart, all your soul, and all your strength" (Deuteronomy 6:5).

LAUGH it UP

WHAT DO YOU MEAN, YOU'LL THINK ABOUT IT? GOD DIDN'T SAY, "THESE ARE THE TEN SUGGESTIONS!"

FAITH walk

Talk about the importance of names. Ask how family members got their names. Look in a book about names and find some names that honor God. For example, Matthew means "gift of God." Does anyone in your family have a name that honors God? Was the name given for that reason or for some other reason? Make new meanings for your names. Include meanings that honor God. For example, "Kylie means 'God's child.' "

CHECK it OUT

Read Psalm 86:11.
How can you show respect for God?

Read Psalm 100:1-2.
What songs do you like to sing to praise God? Sing them as a family.

ARTicles

Using a concordance and a Bible, have your family find all the names used for God, such as Yahweh, Jehovah, the Lord, the Almighty, the Creator, and Abba.

Next, give each family member a thick sheet of paper that's longer and wider than the Bible when it's opened flat. Have family members fold their papers to make protective Bible covers. Then have them use colored markers to write the various names and titles for God on their covers. Place clear Con-Tact paper over the covers to make them last longer.

LESSON 6

GOD'S SPECIAL DAY

THE POINT

We please God by respecting the Lord's day.

THE BIBLE BASIS

Exodus 20:8-11. Keep the Sabbath as a holy day.

God set aside one day each week for us to pause and remember that he's the source and sustainer of all creation. God intended the Sabbath to be different from other days of the week. In the Old Testament, people celebrated the Sabbath on Saturday. Today, most Christians celebrate the Lord's day on Sunday. The Sabbath and the Lord's day aren't exactly the same, but many of the principles God set up for the Sabbath apply to the Lord's day as well.

When we get busy with daily tasks, school, and work, it's easy to forget to think about God. After six days of creative work, God rested. God set apart a day for us to rest from our work and refocus our lives through worship.

Third- and fourth-graders are becoming old enough to recognize that this amazing universe did not just happen by itself. They can value a day set aside to show respect for the awesome God of creation. With the hustle and bustle of chores, homework, soccer on Tuesdays, ballet on Wednesdays, Girl Scouts on Thursdays, and so on, third- and fourth-graders can identify with the need for a designated day of rest. Use this lesson to show your kids that God cares enough for them to provide a day off from their usual pressures so they can worship him.

Other Scriptures used in this lesson are **Isaiah 58:13-14** and **Matthew 12:9-13.**

GETTING THE POINT

Students will

- experience the need for rest,
- identify activities that are restful and relaxing to them,
- connect the Lord's day with worship, and
- discover that helping others is a way to respect the Lord's day.

THIS LESSON AT A GLANCE

Before the lesson, collect the necessary items from the Learning Lab for the activities you plan to use. Refer to the pictures in the margin to see what each item looks like.

SECTION	MINUTES	WHAT STUDENTS WILL DO	LEARNING LAB SUPPLIES	CLASSROOM SUPPLIES
ATTENTION GRABBER	up to 8	**CREATION FATIGUE**—Play a game and experience fatigue.		
BIBLE EXPLORATION AND APPLICATION	up to 15	**SIX PLUS ONE**—Identify whether activities are work or play and read Exodus 20:8-11.	Terry ropes	Bibles, paper, markers, tape, snacks, napkins
	up to 12	**THAT'S AN ORDER!**—Play a game to find out that following commands can be fun and read Isaiah 58:13-14.	Catch ball ring	Bibles
	up to 20	**A SHINING LORD'S DAY**—Read Matthew 12:9-13 and identify ways to help people on the Lord's day.	Cassette: "Sabbath Healing," prism shapes, terry ropes, neon kite string	Bibles, cassette player, pencils, masking tape, index cards
CLOSING	up to 5	**LORD'S DAY CHOICES**—Tell choices they'll make to enjoy the Lord's day.	Straw fan, tool kit	Bible

Hands-On FUN AT HOME

Remember to make photocopies of the "Hands-On Fun at Home" handout (p. 90) to send home with your kids. The "Fun at Home" handout suggests ways for kids to talk with their families about what they're learning in class and helps them put their faith into action.

THE LESSON

As kids arrive, ask them which "Fun at Home" activities they tried. Ask questions such as "What meanings did you discover about your family members' names?" and "What did you like about making Bible book covers?"

Tell kids that whenever you blow the *trumpet* twice, they are to stop talking, raise their hands, and focus on you. Explain that it's important to respond to this signal quickly so the class can do as many fun activities as possible.

ATTENTION GRABBER

CREATION FATIGUE
(up to 8 minutes)

Have kids stand in a circle facing inward. Say: **We're going to play a game called Creation Fatigue. I'll call out the names of some of God's creations. If the creation is above the earth, like a cloud or a bird, stand up and wave your arms over your head.** Demonstrate the action, and have kids follow along. **If the creation is in the sea, like a shark or an octopus, sit down and make swimming motions with your arms.** Demonstrate the action, and have kids follow along. **If the creation is on land, like a tree or a person, stand up and run in place.** Demonstrate the action, and have kids follow along. **Keep doing one motion until I call out the next creation. Let's see how quickly you can do the correct motion.**

Quickly call out these creations:

- **cloud**
- **fish**
- **person**
- **mountain**
- **sun**
- **seaweed**
- **bush**
- **bird**
- **octopus**
- **mosquito**
- **whale**
- **tree**

Keep calling out objects quickly until kids ask you to stop or seem to be getting tired. Then say: **You did a good job trying to keep up. Let's take a couple of deep breaths and sit down.** Have kids sit in a circle. Ask:

- **How do you feel now that this activity is over?** (Tired; exhausted; excited; happy.)
- **When do you get really tired during the week?** (After playing hard; after doing my chores; after a long day of school.)
- **What do you like to do when you're tired?** (Lie down; sit and rest; have a cold drink.)
- **Do you think God ever gets tired? Why or why not?** (No, he's God; no, God is all-powerful; yes, because God has so much to do.)

Say: **God worked hard for six days creating the universe and** everything in it. God rested on the seventh day. God set aside a special day for us to rest and to remember that we belong to him. It comes every seven days. While we are resting and relaxing, God wants us to think about him and all he has done for us.

the POINT

We please God by respecting the Lord's day.

BIBLE EXPLORATION AND APPLICATION

LEARNING LAB

SIX PLUS ONE
(up to 15 minutes)

Before class, make a long line by placing the six *terry ropes* end to end on the floor at a right angle to a wall. Write "Work" on a sheet of paper, and tape it to the wall to the left of the *terry rope* line; write "Play" on a sheet of paper, and tape it to the wall to the right of the line.

Have kids stand on the *terry ropes* in a single file line.

Say: **I'm going to name some activities. If you think the activity is work, jump to the left side of the rope, and shout "work." Jump to the right side of the rope, and shout "play" if you think the activity is play.**

Call out the following activities. Add your own ideas, too, but be sure to include activities that would be work for some people and play for others.

- **swimming**
- **running a race**
- **reading a book**
- **baby-sitting**
- **writing a story**
- **drawing a picture**
- **shooting baskets**
- **taking out the garbage**
- **vacuuming the carpet**
- **brushing the dog or caring for pets**
- **using a computer**
- **practicing a musical instrument**
- **answering all these questions!**

Gather the *terry ropes,* and place them out of sight for use later in this lesson. Have students sit down in a circle. Ask:

- **What did you discover as we played this game?** (There are a lot of things people think are work; not everybody agreed what was work and what was play.)

Say: **We sure have a lot of different ideas about work and play. Let's see what the Bible says about work.**

Distribute Bibles and help kids find **Exodus 20:8-11.** Ask a volunteer to read the passage aloud while others follow along in their Bibles. Ask:

- **What does God say about work?** (Work for six days; relax and rest on the seventh day; remember God on the seventh day.)
- **Why did God set aside a special day for us?** (So we could have a day off; so we would think about what God has made.)
- **At your home, what items are set aside for a special purpose or for special occasions?** (My mom's computer can be used only for

work, not games; I wear my good shoes only to church and on special occasions; we have nice dishes and silverware for when company comes.)

● **Why would you keep things for a special purpose?** (So they'll stay nice; to show it's a special occasion; because my parents say so.)

Say: **We all have things we keep for special times in our lives. God loves us, so he has set aside a special day of rest for us. Let's see how God's special day might work in your life. I'll give you a napkin and seven snack pieces. Group six of them close together. Set the last piece apart. Don't eat any of the pieces until I tell you to.**

Form pairs. Give each person a napkin and seven snack pieces, such as pretzels, chips, or small crackers.

Say: **Let's imagine that each of the snack pieces is a day of the week. The group of six pieces will represent your workweek. The piece that's set apart will represent God's special day. Hold up the first piece of the snack from the group of six. That'll be the first day of your workweek.**

Have partners discuss the following questions. Pause after you ask each question to allow time for discussion. Ask:

● **What kind of work do you usually have to do on the first day of your workweek?** (Go to school; do homework; go to ballet; practice my instrument.)

Say: **Go ahead and eat the first snack piece, then pick up the second snack piece.** Ask:

● **What kind of work do you have to do on the second day of your workweek?**

Continue for each day of the week, and have partners tell what work they have to do, then let them eat the snack for that day. When you get to the seventh piece, say: **Whew! That was a busy week! Now imagine that you're getting ready for the day that God has set aside for rest. I'm going to give you each a sheet of paper and a marker. While you eat the seventh snack piece, write or draw some activities that are restful and relaxing for you.**

TEACHER TIP

It's important to say The Point just as it's written in each activity. Repeating The Point over and over will help kids remember it and apply it to their lives.

Give each person a sheet of paper and a marker. After two minutes, blow the *trumpet* twice, and wait for kids to respond. One at a time, have kids describe their restful and relaxing activities. Post the papers on a bulletin board or wall.

Say: **We have lots of ideas about ways to rest and relax. Maybe you can try some of these ideas today. God has given us six days to do all our work. God set apart the seventh day so we can worship him and relax. We please God by respecting the Lord's day.**

the POINT

THAT'S AN ORDER!
(up to 12 minutes)

LEARNING LAB

As you introduce the next activity, act as if it's going to be something you'll have to force kids to do. In your most "commanding" voice, say:

Now just sit where you are. You're going to have to do an activity. Doing this activity is like following a commandment. You're supposed to follow a commandment whether you like it or not. So, like it or not, here's what you're supposed to do.

> **TEACHER TIP**
>
> Don't let anyone be "It" for longer than one minute. Blow the *trumpet* after one minute. The person holding the ball will be the new It.

Choose one person to be "It," and have everyone else stand in a circle around him or her. Have It wear the *catch ball ring*. Take the ball from the ring, and say: **We're going to play Catch Ball Tag. We'll throw this ball across the circle from person to person. It will try to tag the person who's holding the ball. When It tags a person, that person will become the new It, put on the ring, and stand in the middle. Then the people in the circle will begin tossing the ball again, and the game will continue.**

Toss the ball across the circle to begin the game. After several people have had a chance to be It, blow the *trumpet* twice, and wait for kids to respond. Have kids sit in the circle. Place the *catch ball ring* out of sight for use in later lessons. Ask:

● **When I told you that you *had* to do something, what was your reaction?** (I was scared that it might be something hard or bad; I was worried because I thought it might not be fun.)

● **How do you feel when you're commanded to do something in real life?** (Mad, because it's probably something that's awful to do; disappointed, because it's something I probably wouldn't do if I had a choice.)

● **What surprised you about this activity?** (It was fun even though you said we had to do it; some things we're told to do turn out better than we think they will.)

Say: **Sometimes we don't want to do what we're told to do. But rules are usually for our own good. And sometimes, like in our game, we discover we actually enjoy following the commands! Let's discover some ways we can enjoy God's command to rest one day a week.**

> **TEACHER TIP**
>
> Encourage active participation by following up kids' answers with questions such as "What did you mean by that?" and "Can you tell me more?"

Form trios. Help kids find **Isaiah 58:13-14.** Explain that the book of Isaiah is just a little past the middle of the Bible. Have kids take turns reading the Bible passage in their trios. Then have them discuss the following questions. Pause after you ask each question to allow time for discussion. Ask:

● **After reading the passage, what do you think God wants us to do on the Lord's day?** (Remember God; do good things; be glad God exists.)

● **What are some different kinds of things we can do on the Lord's day to show we remember God?** (Go to church; pray; sing songs; give thanks; go for a hike in God's creation; spend time with our families.)

Blow the *trumpet* twice, and wait for kids to respond. Invite them to share insights from their discussions.

the POINT

Say: **God wants us to rest, worship, and remember him on the Lord's day. We can enjoy worship by singing, praying, and thanking God for all he does for us. We please God by respecting the Lord's day.**

A SHINING LORD'S DAY
(up to 20 minutes)

LEARNING LAB

Say: **God wants us to set aside one day each week to honor him. People in Jesus' day celebrated the Sabbath on Saturday. Most Christians today celebrate the Lord's day on Sunday to help them remember Jesus' resurrection. The Sabbath and the Lord's day aren't exactly the same, but many of the things the Bible teaches about the Sabbath apply to our Lord's day as well. Let's hear about a way Jesus honored God on the Sabbath.**

Play the "Sabbath Healing" segment of the *cassette tape.* In this segment, two Pharisees try to catch Jesus healing on the Sabbath. The segment is based on **Luke 13:10-21.**

Stop the tape, then say: **Imagine that it's Sunday. You cut your arm badly, and you go to the emergency room. Blood is pouring out of your arm, and the doctor says to you, "Come back on Monday. I don't work today because I respect the Lord's day."** Ask:

- **What would you say?** (Help me—I'm going to bleed to death before Monday; I need help now, not tomorrow; it's OK to help people on the Lord's day.)
- **How would this situation be like Jesus' healing the woman with the crippled back?** (The woman wanted help as soon as possible; Jesus knew the woman needed help right then.)

Say: **Jesus respected the Sabbath, but he knew it was OK for him to heal the woman.** Distribute Bibles and help kids find **Matthew 12:9-13.** When everyone has found the passage, ask a volunteer to read it aloud. Ask:

- **What did Jesus say is lawful to do on the Sabbath?** (Good things; heal people; help people.)

Form groups of no more than four. Distribute the *prism shapes* so that each group has the same number of shapes. Have each group choose a recorder, reporter, and encouragers. Give each recorder a pencil, a strip of masking tape, and the same number of index cards as *prism shapes.*

Say: **The *prism shapes* remind us of the Lord's day. It should be the sparkling star of the week, a day we look forward to. We respect the Lord's day as we rest, relax, remember God, and help others in need.**

Helping others is a way to show respect for God and God's creations. In your groups, think of good deeds you could do on the Lord's day as a way of showing respect to God. Think of one good deed for each *prism shape.* For example, a good deed could be to volunteer to serve in a homeless shelter or to bake cookies and deliver them to a nursing home. Recorders, write one idea per index card, then tape a *prism shape* to each card. Encouragers, urge group members to think of ideas. Reporters, read your group's ideas to the class when I give the signal.

While groups are working, hang the six *terry ropes* from a bulletin board, wall, or doorway. Hang one 6-foot length of *neon kite string* beside the sixth *terry rope.*

After three minutes, blow the *trumpet* twice, and wait for kids to respond. Have kids gather near the hanging *terry ropes.*

Say: **God set the Lord's day apart from other days of the week. We can honor God on the Lord's day by relaxing, worshiping God, and helping others in need. The six *terry ropes* represent the six days of our work week. The *neon kite string* represents the Lord's day.**

the POINT

Have reporters read their groups' good deeds. As reporters share each idea, have them tape that index card to the *neon kite string.* After all reporters have done this, say: **We can make the Lord's day shine by resting, worshiping, and doing good deeds. We please God by respecting the Lord's day.**

Leave the *terry ropes, neon kite string,* and index cards with *prism shapes* hanging as a visual reminder of the lesson. Put them away after class for use in future lessons.

Hands-On FUN AT HOME

We believe that Christian education extends beyond the classroom into the home. Photocopy the "Hands-On Fun at Home" handout (p. 90) for this week, and send it home with your kids. Encourage kids to try several activities and discuss the Bible verses and questions with their parents.

CLOSING

LEARNING LAB

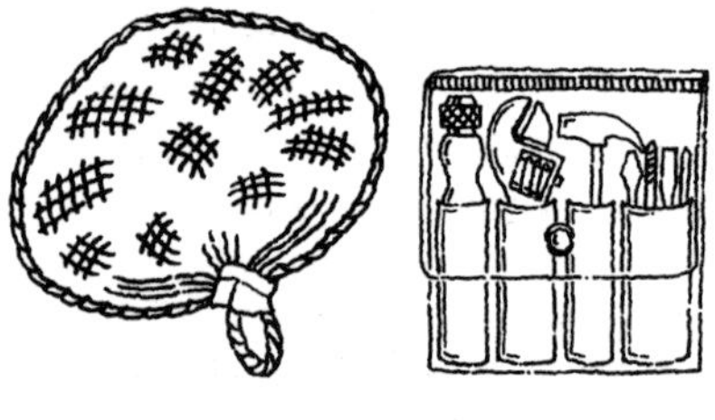

LORD'S DAY CHOICES
(up to 5 minutes)

Set out the *straw fan,* the *tool kit* with the hammer lying on top, and an open Bible. Gather kids in a circle around the items.

the POINT

Say: **God gave us the Lord's day as a gift so we could rest and relax** (pick up the *straw fan,* fan yourself, then put it back down), **so we could worship and enjoy God** (pick up the open Bible, run your fingers under a line of print, then put it back down), **and so we could help others** (pick up the hammer from the *tool kit,* hammer three times, then put it back down). **We please God by respecting the Lord's day. One at a time, each of you can stand in the center of the circle. We'll say,** "(Name), **God gave you the gift of the Lord's day." You'll respond to the affirmation by saying, "I can keep the Lord's day by..." Then pick up one of the objects and say one activity you'll do this week. For example, you could fan yourself and say you'll rest and relax.**

LESSON 7

TOGETHER FOREVER

THE POINT

We please God by treating our families right.

THE BIBLE BASIS

Exodus 20:12, 14. Don't commit adultery; honor your parents.

Did you know that "Honor your father and your mother" is a two-part commandment? If you honor your parents, the Bible says "you will live a long time." According to Israelite law, if you didn't honor your parents, you could be put to death (Exodus 21:17). Honoring parents is more than recognizing the wonderful things they do. Honoring parents and maintaining right relationships with family members is a way to acknowledge that God made all people and we can all be God's children.

For some third- and fourth-graders, honoring parents is a normal part of family life. But other third- and fourth-graders have difficulty with the commandment because they may not recognize that their parents have acted in ways that deserve honor. Kids need to know that we are all children of God through our faith in Christ. God gives us families to take care of us and maintain our gift of life. When we honor our parents, we're really honoring God. Use this lesson to help third- and fourth-graders see that honoring parents is a way to honor God.

Other Scriptures used in this lesson are **Matthew 5:23-24; 7:12; 1 Corinthians 13:4-7;** and **Ephesians 6:2-3.**

TEACHER TIP

Be sensitive to kids who may be abused by their parents. It may be difficult or impossible for them to think of honoring their abusive parents. Listen to these children and respect their feelings. If you suspect abuse, talk with your pastor about appropriate intervention.

Encourage kids who are adopted or who live with step-parents, grandparents, or other care givers to honor the family members who are currently caring for them.

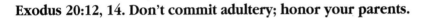

GETTING THE POINT

Students will

- explore feelings that result when families don't get along,
- examine what happens when there are problems in families,
- express appreciation for family members, and
- discover ways to treat family members with respect.

THIS LESSON AT A GLANCE

Before the lesson, collect the necessary items from the Learning Lab for the activities you plan to use. Refer to the pictures in the margin to see what each item looks like.

SECTION	MINUTES	WHAT STUDENTS WILL DO	LEARNING LAB SUPPLIES	CLASSROOM SUPPLIES
ATTENTION GRABBER	up to 5	**STOP THAT FIGHTING!**—Have a pretend fight with paper balls.	Paper balls	
BIBLE EXPLORATION AND APPLICATION	up to 15	**A REWARDING COMMANDMENT**—Read Ephesians 6:2-3 and affirm family members.	Miniature trophy	Bibles, masking tape
	up to 20	**FAMILY WORK TIME**—Work in family groups to complete chores and read 1 Corinthians 13:4-7.		Bibles, cleaning supplies
	up to 15	**LEAVE IT AT THE ALTAR**—Eat snacks, read Matthew 5:23-24 and 7:12, and forgive each other.	Cassette: "Music for Making Peace"	Bibles, cassette player, snacks
CLOSING	up to 5	**REMEMBER!**—Tie strings around their fingers to remember how to treat their families.	Neon kite string	Scissors

Hands-On FUN AT HOME

Remember to make photocopies of the "Hands-On Fun at Home" handout (p. 100) to send home with your kids. The "Fun at Home" handout suggests ways for kids to talk with their families about what they're learning in class and helps them put their faith into action.

THE LESSON

LEARNING LAB

As kids arrive, ask them which "Fun at Home" activities they tried. Ask questions such as "In what ways did you enjoy the Lord's day with your family?" and "What kind of homemade instruments did you use for your praise songs?"

Tell kids that whenever you blow the *trumpet* twice, they are to stop talking, raise their hands, and focus on you. Explain that it's important to respond to this signal quickly so the class can do as many fun activities as possible.

ATTENTION GRABBER

STOP THAT FIGHTING!
(up to 5 minutes)

LEARNING LAB

Hand out all the *paper balls*. Say: **We're going to have a fight with the *paper balls*. Here are the rules: You can throw only *paper balls*. Aim below the neck. Once you throw all your *paper balls*, you can pick up balls from the floor and throw them. Imagine the other kids are your brothers and sisters. I'll give you the signal when it's time to stop. Ready, set, throw!**

After about two minutes, blow the *trumpet* twice, and wait for kids to respond. Have them pick up the *paper balls* and sit down in a circle. Gather the *paper balls*, and place them out of sight for use in future lessons. Ask:

- **What was it like to fight during this activity?** (It was fun to be able to throw things at other kids; I don't like to fight; I hated it because someone kept throwing just at me.)
- **How was this activity like what happens when family members don't get along?** (Sometimes it seems as if we fight for no reason; it can feel as though everyone's against you.)
- **How does it feel when families don't get along?** (Frustrating; sad; angry; lonely.)

Say: **We don't always get along with our families. Sometimes we experience unhappy times and we fight. At other times, we enjoy each other. God gave us our family members, and he wants us to treat them with care and respect. We please God by treating our families right.**

> **TEACHER TIP**
>
> If possible, play this game in an area such as a fellowship hall or large meeting room. If your classroom is small, have everyone sit on the floor to "fight."

the POINT

BIBLE EXPLORATION AND APPLICATION

LEARNING LAB

A REWARDING COMMANDMENT
(up to 15 minutes)

Say: **God gave us two commandments about families. Let's learn about one of them now.**

Distribute Bibles and help kids look up **Exodus 20:14.** Have a volunteer read the verse aloud while others follow along in their Bibles. Say: **Adultery means not being true to your husband or wife. Married people obey this commandment by loving and staying with the person they married.** Ask:

● **What happens when people break this commandment?** (They get a divorce; it's hard for their families.)

● **Why do you think God gave us a commandment like this?** (Because it's important for parents to love each other and stay together; because God loves us and wants us to have happy families.)

Say: **When people get married, they make a promise to love each other and stay together. Sometimes parents divorce and live in different places. That's not your fault. Parents make their own choices. God loves you just the same. Now let's look at God's other commandment about families.**

Help kids look up **Exodus 20:12** in their Bibles. Have a volunteer read the verse aloud. Next, help kids find **Ephesians 6:2-3.** Have a volunteer read the verses aloud while others follow along in their Bibles.

Have kids stand, then say: **Raise your hands when you've thought of an answer to each of the questions I'm about to ask. I'd like to hear lots of different, interesting answers. When someone gives an answer you've thought of and you don't have anything more to add, you may sit down. When everyone is seated, I'll ask you to stand again for the next question.** Ask:

● **Why do you think God wants us to honor our parents?** (Families are important; God designed families to care for each other; God created parents.)

● **Why do you think God says everything will go well for us if we follow this commandment?** (God really wants us to follow it; maybe God thinks we won't do it if we don't get a reward.)

● **Do we get rewards for following God's other commandments? Explain.** (Yes, we have a better life if we follow God's commandments; no, the other commandments don't say anything about getting a reward; God's love is the reward for following God's commandments.)

Say: **We are all children of God through our faith in Christ. God gives us families to take care of us. When we honor our parents, we're really honoring God.**

Form trios. Say: **You'll need masking tape for the next part of our lesson. Each of you should take as much tape as you think you might need.**

Take a 15- to 20-inch piece of tape for yourself. Then pass the roll of tape around. Don't tell kids how much they'll need. After everyone has masking tape, say: **It's good for families to stick together and do things for one another. In your trios, you're going to share about good things family members do for you. Wind the tape so it goes around your hand. For each time you wind the tape, name a family member, and tell one thing that person does to take care of you.**

Demonstrate by wrapping the tape and saying something like "My son takes out the garbage so that we can have a healthy, bug-free home."

After four minutes, blow the *trumpet* twice, and wait for kids to respond. Say: **Now unwrap the masking tape slowly. For each time the tape unwraps, name one way you take care of family members. When you finish unwrapping, make the tape into a little ball.**

Demonstrate by unwrapping the tape from your hand and saying something like "I make sure my kids have snacks to eat after school" or "write weekly encouraging notes to my grandmother."

After four minutes, blow the *trumpet* twice, and wait for kids to respond. Have kids stand in a large circle. Say: **Keep your tape ball as a reminder that families need to stick together and do helpful things for each other.**

Bring out the *miniature trophy,* and say: **A trophy represents a champion or a winner. I'll pass this trophy around the circle. When it comes to you, say how one or more of your family members is a champion in your life. For example, you could say, "My stepmom is a champion because she always listens to me, even when she's busy," or "My sister is a champion because she lets me borrow her bike whenever I want." Then pass the trophy to the person on your right. We'll go around the circle until everyone has had a turn.**

After everyone has had a turn, hold the trophy, and say: **Our families do many things to care for us. Honoring our family members is a way to honor God. We please God by treating our families right.**

Place the *miniature trophy* out of sight for use in future lessons.

TEACHER TIP

If kids have taken very short pieces of tape, have them wrap the tape around their little fingers. Kids with very long pieces might have to think of many ways to share or wrap the tape around their feet or legs.

TEACHER TIP

It's important to say The Point just as it's written during each activity. Repeating The Point over and over will help kids remember it and apply it to their lives.

the POINT

FAMILY WORK TIME
(up to 20 minutes)

Before kids arrive, arrange for them to do three jobs around the church. For example:

- Job 1: Vacuum the carpet.
- Job 2: Dust the furniture.
- Job 3: Wash some windows.

For each job, include only one set of cleaning supplies so group

TEACHER TIP

If it's nice outside, you could have the three groups do three outside jobs, such as sweep the sidewalk, wash outside windows, and rake the grass.

TEACHER TIP

It's OK if some family groups are larger than others, since families in real life come in various sizes!

TEACHER TIP

Visit the groups and observe their projects in progress. Note the comments they make about sharing supplies and who the bosses are. Refer to the comments during the upcoming discussion.

members have to share. For example, include only one dust cloth instead of four or five. The object is for kids to share and get along "as a family."

Say: **Let's form three groups by birth months. Imagine your group is a family. After I describe all the families, find your group and sit in a circle. Everybody with birthdays from January through April is in the first family. Everybody with birthdays from May through August is in the second family. Everybody with birthdays from September through December is in the third family.**

Wait until kids are each sitting in a circle with a family group. Blow the *trumpet* twice, and wait for kids to respond.

Say: **In a minute, we're going to complete family jobs around the church. But first, tell me what jobs you do at home.** (Take out the trash; feed the dog; clean my room.)

Say: **Before we do family jobs around the church, decide what role each person will play in your family. Besides the roles of mom, dad, brother, or sister, you can have stepparents, grandparents, aunts, uncles, and cousins.**

After one minute, blow the *trumpet* twice, and wait for kids to respond. Assign each group one of the three jobs you've prepared. Send kids off to complete their projects. Make sure kids will stay in safe areas and won't disturb others.

After 10 minutes, blow the *trumpet* twice, and have kids gather back in the meeting room and sit in a large circle. Ask:

- **What was your reaction to the role you played in your family?** (I was frustrated because nobody listened to "the baby"; I didn't like taking orders from anyone; it was fun working together.)
- **What happened in your family as you worked on your job?** (Nobody could agree on who would use the supplies; our family got along, and we had fun trying to work together; everybody wanted to be in charge.)
- **How is this like what happens in real families?** (Some families enjoy working together; some family members are never happy about family decisions; some families laugh a lot, some families argue a lot.)
- **What happens when there are problems in families?** (People get their feelings hurt; people get mad; people don't seem to care; people outside the family may notice that the family doesn't get along.)
- **When families have problems, what do you think God wants them to do?** (Work out their problems; try to see problems from other people's point of view; try to be fair to everybody.)

Say: **I could have made your jobs a bit easier. I could have given you each your own set of supplies so you wouldn't have had to share. But I deliberately gave you only one set of supplies so you'd get the true feeling of family teamwork. Let's look up a Bible passage that tells us about something we should share with our families.**

Distribute Bibles and help kids find **1 Corinthians 13:4-7.** Ask a volunteer to read it aloud while others follow along in their Bibles. Have kids discuss the following questions in their family groups. Pause after you ask each question to allow time for discussion.

Ask:

● **Did your family group show any of these characteristics of love as you did your job?** (No, we were rude to one another; no, our family members insisted on their own way; yes, people were patient and kind and helpful.)

● **Would you like to be treated in any of these ways? Explain.** (I like people to be patient with me because I feel bad when they aren't; I don't like people to be rude to me because it hurts my feelings; I like it when people tell me the truth because then I know what's what.)

● **What would your family be like if you always treated each other in the good ways listed in the Bible passage?** (My life would be nicer; it would be the same because we try to do that now.)

Blow the *trumpet* twice, and wait for kids to respond. Invite them to share insights from their discussions.

the POINT

Say: **God has given us commandments to help us live better lives. God wants us to treat family members in a loving way. We please God by treating our families right. Treating family members right is a way to honor God.**

LEAVE IT AT THE ALTAR
(up to 15 minutes)

LEARNING LAB

Serve a snack. As you hand out snacks, serve one family group, and refuse to serve the others. To the groups you refuse to serve, make comments such as "You can't have any," "This is all mine," and "Why should I share with you? Would you share with me?" Be overly dramatic and talk in a childish manner so kids know it's an act!

When you've finished serving the snack, ask:

● **How did you feel about the way I served the snacks?** (It wasn't very nice; I thought it was funny that you were acting that way; I expected you to share with everyone.)

● **Do family members ever treat each other as I treated some people in class? Why or why not?** (Yes, they play favorites; yes, they say ugly things and are mean for no good reason; no, some families try to be nice to each other.)

● **How do you like family members to treat you?** (Nice; like they like me; I want them to share with me.)

Give snacks to the groups you didn't serve earlier, and say: **Our class is like a family, so I should treat everyone fairly. Here's a snack for you.**

Say: **You've all probably heard of the verse called the Golden Rule. Let's look at that verse together.** Distribute Bibles and help kids find **Matthew 7:12.** Ask a volunteer to read the verse aloud. Ask:

● **How does this verse remind you of what happened when I gave the snacks to the people who didn't get them before?** (Everyone was treated fairly; you'd probably like to be treated right, so you started to treat everyone else right.)

Say: **Let's ask God to help us remember to treat our families right. In your family groups, think of what we should say in our prayer.**

After about 20 seconds, blow the *trumpet* twice, and wait for kids to respond. Say: **Wait! We can't offer a prayer to God yet! We have to do something else first!**

Help kids find **Matthew 5:23-24.** Have them read the passage in their family groups. Ask:

● **What does this passage tell us to do?** (To make up with a sister or brother before we worship God; to tell people we're sorry before we go to church.)

● **How important is it to make things right with family members? Explain.** (Very important, because we should be right with others before worshiping God; important, because God wants us to make up with family members first.)

● **What are some ways to make peace with family members?** (Apologize; ask for forgiveness; give back what we took from them; do something special for them.)

Say: **Jesus thought it was so important for us to treat our families right that he said we should make things right with them before we worship God. Let's "make things right" with any members of our group who we didn't treat right so far today. Shake hands with members of your group.**

Play the "Music for Making Peace" segment of the *cassette tape* as kids affirm each other. Wait until everyone has made peace, then stop the cassette. Blow the *trumpet* twice, and wait for kids to respond.

Say: **Now that we've made peace with others, we can offer our prayer to God.**

Have kids join hands in a large circle, bow their heads, and offer some ideas about making peace that they thought of in their family groups. Then pray: **God, please help us remember ways to treat our families right. Thanks for families who care for us. Thanks for your forgiveness and love. Amen.**

Say: **We should treat our families the way we wish to be treated—with patience and kindness. We please God by treating our families right.**

> **TEACHER TIP**
>
> Sometimes the most sensitive children have the most insensitive family situations. These children can feel tremendous guilt for their warring, shouting, raging families. Say: **Sometimes it's out of our control when parents or siblings fight. We need to do the best we can to be loving and forgiving. Then we can pray and put our family members in God's hands.**

the POINT

Hands-On FUN AT HOME

We believe that Christian education extends beyond the classroom into the home. Photocopy the "Hands-On Fun at Home" handout (p. 100) for this week, and send it home with your kids. Encourage kids to try several activities and discuss the Bible verses and questions with their parents.

LEARNING LAB

REMEMBER!
(up to 5 minutes)

Have kids sit in a circle on the floor. Give everyone an 8-inch piece of *neon kite string*.

Say: **Sometimes people tie strings around their fingers to remind them to do something important. Let's go around the circle and each say one thing we want to remember to do to treat our families right. For example, you could say, "Tell my parents I love them," or "Be patient with my little sister." After you share your idea, have someone sitting next to you help you tie the string on your right pointer finger as a reminder to follow up on your idea this week.**

Have each person in the circle share an idea. Make sure kids tie the strings loosely—not too tight! After all kids have string tied around their fingers, offer a prayer asking God to give kids patience and to help them treat their families right.

the POINT

Then say: **God will help us because we please God by treating our families right.**

Hands-On FUN AT HOME

LESSON 7:
TOGETHER FOREVER

the POINT **We please God by treating our families right.**

BIBLE FOCUS

"Love the Lord your God with all your heart, all your soul, and all your strength" (Deuteronomy 6:5).

FAMILY appreciation CALENDAR

Here's a month of nice things to do for family members. Hang it on your refrigerator door. Have family members place a check in the square when they complete each idea.					**1/2** Put an "I love you" note on someone's bed.
3 Do someone else's chores.	**4** Give back something you borrowed.	**5** Let someone else pick a TV program to watch.	**6** Offer to clean up after dinner.	**7** Read a story to someone.	**8/9** Tell a family member three things you like about him or her.
10 Share a favorite Bible verse.	**11** Listen without interrupting.	**12** Teach someone a happy song.	**13** Put a happy message in someone's lunch sack.	**14** Write a thank you note to whoever fixed meals today.	**15/16** Tell someone a funny joke.
17 Tuck someone in bed tonight.	**18** Help someone put away his or her things.	**19** Play a game someone else chooses.	**20** Shine someone's shoes. Give someone a hug.	**21** Tell someone, "I love you."	**22/23** Help someone find something he or she has lost.
24 Smile.	**25** Help someone complete his or her chores.	**26** Tell family members why they're important to you.	**27** Set the table for dinner.	**28** Take a walk with a family member.	**29/30** Share a possession.

LAUGH it UP

I LIKE TO DO NICE THINGS FOR MY FAMILY...
...IT MAKES THEM WONDER WHAT I'M UP TO!

CHECK it OUT

Read Psalm 119:1-3.

Why do you think God wants us to treat our families right? What happy things happen in families when people try to treat one another with respect?

Read John 15:12.

What can you do this week to love family members as God loves you?

LESSON 8

GOD-PLEASING ACTIONS

THE POINT

We please God with our actions.

THE BIBLE BASIS

Exodus 20:13, 15-16. Don't kill, steal, or lie.

God cares how we treat one another. Through the commandments against killing, stealing, and lying, God demands universal respect for life, people, property, and reputations. Each person's life comes from God. We must treat others with the honesty and respect they deserve.

Third- and fourth-graders are well-acquainted with the commandments against killing, stealing, and lying. Every day, television portrays the breaking of all three of these commandments. Unfortunately, these actions are becoming common behavior. Use this lesson to help third- and fourth-graders understand that God commands us to respect all life, as well as people's property, their trust, and their reputations.

Other Scriptures used in this lesson are **Proverbs 29:27; Jeremiah 7:8-10;** and **James 1:19-21.**

GETTING THE POINT

Students will

- discuss pleasing actions,
- experience a tangled web of lies,
- identify things besides money or objects that can be stolen, and
- examine appropriate ways to handle angry feelings and differences.

THIS LESSON AT A GLANCE

Before the lesson, collect the necessary items from the Learning Lab for the activities you plan to use. Refer to the pictures in the margin to see what each item looks like.

SECTION	MINUTES	WHAT STUDENTS WILL DO	LEARNING LAB SUPPLIES	CLASSROOM SUPPLIES
ATTENTION GRABBER	up to 10	**PLEASING PICTURES**—Try to identify pictures of actions that please God.		Newsprint, markers
BIBLE EXPLORATION AND APPLICATION	up to 15	**WEB OF LIES**—Create a string web as they tell a story of lies, then read Exodus 20:16; Proverbs 29:27; and Jeremiah 7:8-10.	Neon kite string	Bibles
	up to 15	**STEAL THE JEWELS**—Play a pretend stealing game and read Exodus 20:15.	Gift box, paper balls	Bibles
	up to 15	**HELP! GUNS KILL!**—Listen to interviews and read Exodus 20:13 and James 1:19-21.	Cassette: "Guns in School"	Bibles, cassette player
CLOSING	up to 5	**WEB OF LOVE**—Grab wrists across a circle and express love for one another.		

Remember to make photocopies of the "Hands-On Fun at Home" handout (p. 109) to send home with your kids. The "Fun at Home" handout suggests ways for kids to talk with their families about what they're learning in class and helps them put their faith into action.

THE LESSON

LEARNING LAB

As kids arrive, ask them which "Fun at Home" activities they tried. Ask questions such as "What nice things did you do for your family members last week?" and "What did you learn from the Bible passages about treating your family with respect?"

Tell kids that whenever you blow the *trumpet* twice, they are to stop talking, raise their hands, and focus on you. Explain that it's important to respond to this signal quickly so the class can do as many fun activities as possible.

ATTENTION GRABBER

PLEASING PICTURES
(up to 10 minutes)

Form two teams and give each team a marker. Hang several sheets of newsprint on a wall. Say: **We're going to start our class today by playing a game of Pleasing Pictures. One at a time, each team will choose a person to come to the newsprint and draw a picture of an action that's pleasing to God. I'll whisper to that person what to draw. Stick figures are great for this game because you can draw them fast and your team will have more time to guess. You will have one minute to guess what action each drawing represents. After a minute, if no one has guessed the picture, the drawer must say what it is. Then the other team will take a turn.**

I'll count the number of guesses each team takes. At the end of the game, the team with fewer guesses wins. Let's practice one first.

Go to the newsprint and draw a person praying. Have kids take turns guessing. Count the number of guesses until someone gets it right or until one minute is up.

Have the first team choose a person to draw. Whisper to the drawer one of the following actions. Count the guesses, then let the other team try. Continue down the list, keeping a record of each team's guesses on a separate sheet of newsprint. After about eight minutes, be sure that each team has had an equal number of tries, then total each team's guesses and have everyone clap for the team with fewer guesses. Here are the actions:

- **giving food to a needy person**
- **visiting a sick person**
- **reading the Bible**
- **listening to a sermon**
- **hugging a parent**
- **singing a hymn or song**
- **mowing an elderly person's lawn**
- **gladly putting money in the offering basket at church**

TEACHER TIP

Some third- and fourth-grade students are sensitive about their artistic abilities. Your example in this activity can help lessen students' anxieties—especially if you're not an accomplished artist!

TEACHER TIP

If you have a large class, form more teams. Have each team choose a guess counter, a timer, and a list keeper who will whisper the actions. Copy the list of pleasing actions on separate sheets of paper, and give each list keeper a copy.

After eight minutes, blow the *trumpet* twice, and wait for kids to respond. Have everyone sit in a circle on the floor. Ask:

● **Why do you think the actions we drew are pleasing to God?** (They help people; they show love; they give to people who need it.)

● **What other pleasing actions can you think of?** (Being nice to new kids; saying nice things to people; being kind and helping younger brothers or sisters with their homework.)

● **How do you think God feels when we do nice things for others?** (Happy; pleased with us; glad we're treating people nicely.)

the POINT ☞

Say: **God gave us the Ten Commandments to tell us some actions that he does and doesn't like. When we follow the Ten Commandments, ☞ we please God with our actions.**

BIBLE EXPLORATION AND APPLICATION

LEARNING LAB

WEB OF LIES
(up to 15 minutes)

Have kids stand in a circle. Wrap one end of the *neon kite string* around your hand, and begin to unroll it.

Say: **We're going to string out a story about a tangled web of lies. I'll start a story about telling a lie, then I'll hold one end of the string and toss the rest of it to someone else. That person will add to the story, hold a section of the string, then toss the rest of it to another person, and so on. We'll keep going until everyone has added to the web of lies and is holding a section of the string. Here's how our story starts: Once upon a time, I forgot to do my homework, but I told my mom I'd already done it.**

Hold one end of the string, then toss the rest of it to someone across the circle so that person can continue the story.

After everyone is tangled up and has added a lie to the story, ask:

● **What was it like to make up lies during this activity?** (It was hard to think of what to say; I didn't like telling lies even though I was supposed to.)

● **What happened to us as we did this activity?** (We got tangled in the string; our lies got wilder and more unbelievable.)

● **How is what happened to us like what happens when you tell lies in real life?** (The story and the string got more and more tangled; the more lies you tell, the more complicated everything gets.)

Say: **Let's get untangled from our web of lies and look at what the Bible says about lying. The last person who contributed to our story will start first. Say a word that describes how people might feel when they get tangled up in a web of lies. As you say the word, rewind the string toward the next person who's holding it. Then that person will say a word, and so on, until our *neon kite string* is**

TEACHER TIP

If kids need ideas, you could suggest: **The next day, I told my teacher I lost my homework. Then my teacher called my mom, so I told my mom that I found my homework but the dog tore it up.**

rewound. It's OK to say the same word more than once.

Place the *neon kite string* out of sight for use in future lessons. Say: **One of the Ten Commandments talks about lying.** Distribute Bibles and help kids find **Exodus 20:16.** Have a volunteer read it aloud while others follow along in their Bibles. Ask:

- **What could happen if you tell lies about people?** (They could get punished for something they didn't do; you could ruin their reputations.)
- **What do you think about people who lie to you?** (I can't trust them; I always wonder if they're telling me the truth or a lie.)

Say: **Let's read some other verses that deal with lying.** Help kids find **Proverbs 29:27.** Have someone read the verse aloud. Then, help kids find **Jeremiah 7:8-10,** and have someone read that passage aloud. Ask:

- **What do you think honest people think about dishonest people?** (They can't trust them; dishonest people try to cheat others.)
- **What would life be like if people couldn't trust you?** (I could tell the truth and they wouldn't believe it; I would feel bad because people wouldn't like me.)
- **What does God think about telling lies?** (He doesn't want people to lie; God says it will ruin our lives.)
- **How do you feel when people trust you?** (Happy, because people know I can be a good friend; like I'm a valuable person.)

Say: **It feels good to be able to trust people and know that other people trust you. When you tell the truth, people know they can trust you. Telling the truth pleases God. When we tell the truth, we please God with our actions.**

> ### TEACHER TIP
> It's important to say The Point just as it's written in each activity. Repeating The Point over and over will help kids remember it and apply it to their lives.

the POINT

STEAL THE JEWELS
(up to 15 minutes)

LEARNING LAB

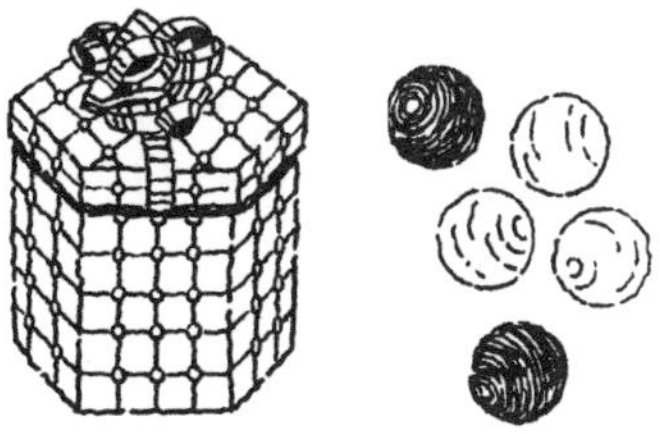

Place several *paper balls* in the *gift box.* Hold the box so kids can see the *paper balls.* Say: **In a minute, we'll play a game, and we'll all try to steal these precious jewels.**

Have kids stand in a circle about 10 feet across. Choose one person to be "It" and place the jewels at his or her feet.

Say: **When I say, "Steal the jewels," run up to It and try to grab the jewels. But be careful—if It touches you, you're frozen until the end of the game. If you manage to steal the jewels and get back to your place in the circle, then you get to be It and a new game starts. Ready? Steal the jewels!**

After a few rounds, blow the *trumpet* twice, and wait for kids to respond. Ask:

- **What was it like to try to steal the jewels?** (Fun; exciting; bad, because I got caught.)
- **What was it like going after the jewels, knowing you might get caught?** (It was scary; there was a chance I could grab them without getting caught.)
- **How is that like when you're tempted to steal or do something**

> ### TEACHER TIP
> If you have more than 20 kids, form another circle. Make another jewel container by placing the *prism shapes* in a *plastic egg.*

TEACHER TIP

If kids have trouble stealing the jewels, hint that they can all go for It at once. Most of the kids will get frozen, but someone is bound to get through.

wrong in life? (I want to do it, but I'm afraid I might get caught; I know it's wrong, and I know I shouldn't do it.)

Say: **This was just a game and wasn't real stealing. Stealing doesn't please God. Let's read what the Bible says about stealing.**

Form pairs. Help them find **Exodus 20:15.** Have everyone read the verse in unison. Then have partners discuss the following questions. Pause after you ask each question to allow time for discussion. Ask:

- **What are some things people steal?** (Money; cars; jewelry; pencils; books.)
- **What are some things besides objects that people might steal?** (Time; homework answers; reputations.)

Say: **Objects aren't our only valuables. Our time is valuable, too.** Ask:

- **How can you steal time from someone?** (By staying at a person's house too long; by not coming when my mother calls me; by staying on the phone when someone else needs to use it.)

Say: **Other valuable things people sometimes steal are answers for tests or homework.** Ask:

- **Why shouldn't you steal homework answers?** (It's wrong; it's cheating; it's stealing people's chance to learn for themselves; I might be stealing my own chance to learn.)
- **What are some of the dangers of stealing?** (Whatever we steal may be really important to the person it's stolen from; if we steal once, we're more likely to do it again; God doesn't want us to steal.)

Blow the *trumpet* twice, and wait for kids to respond. Invite them to share insights from their discussions.

the POINT

Say: **God wants us to respect other people. God wants us to respect their possessions, time, opportunities, reputations, and chances to learn. When we steal, we aren't respecting them as the special people God created them to be. When we respect others, we please God with our actions.**

LEARNING LAB

HELP! GUNS KILL!
(up to 15 minutes)

Say: **Lying and stealing aren't the only actions that don't please God. Every day we read in the newspapers or hear on the news about kidnapping, drive-by shootings, and other violent actions. Those actions don't please God, and they often hurt innocent people. Let's listen to a news report about how violence is affecting kids in school.**

Play the "Guns in School" segment of the *cassette tape.* This segment is a news-style report about school violence.

After the segment, stop the tape, and ask:

- **How did you feel as you listened to the tape?** (Scared; surprised; worried.)

● **What's scary about kids bringing weapons to school?** (They might use them; somebody could get hurt or killed.)

Say: **Now let's take a look at the commandment against murder.** Help kids find **Exodus 20:13.** Ask everyone to read it aloud together.

Have kids stand, then say: **Raise your hand when you've thought of an answer to each of the questions I'm about to ask. I'd like to hear lots of different, interesting answers. When someone gives an answer you've thought of and you don't have anything more to add, you may sit down. When everyone is seated, I'll ask you to stand again for the next question.** Ask:

● **When you watch television or read the newspapers, what reasons do people give for killing each other?** (Hate; anger; jealousy; it was an accident.)

● **How do you feel when you hear about killing and murder?** (Scared it might happen to me or someone I love; like the world is out of control.)

● **Does killing someone solve problems? Why or why not?** (No, it just makes more problems; no, there will always be somebody else that a person doesn't like.)

● **Why did God command us not to kill?** (Because God made all life; people are God's creations, and it's not right to kill them; God loves people and doesn't want them hurt or murdered.)

Say: **People kill because they get angry or because they feel hate. But God has a better plan for his world.**

Help kids find **James 1:19-21** and have someone read the passage aloud. Ask:

● **How would our world be different if people followed the advice in this passage?** (I'd feel better because I wouldn't be scared if someone got angry; nobody would get murdered; people would treat everyone nice.)

● **What are ways, other than killing, to deal with hate and misunderstandings?** (Sit down and talk; learn why someone is different; think of other ways to get what you want.)

Say: **God wants people to care for one another and to respect his creations. God created us with brains to think of ways to work out problems. We show we respect life when we refuse to hate and kill. When we respect others' lives, we please God with our actions.**

the POINT

Hands-On FUN AT HOME

We believe that Christian education extends beyond the classroom into the home. Photocopy the "Hands-On Fun at Home" handout (p. 109) for this week, and send it home with your kids. Encourage kids to try several activities and discuss the Bible verses and questions with their parents.

CLOSING

WEB OF LOVE
(up to 5 minutes)

Have kids form a circle. Say: **Earlier we created a web of lies. Now let's form a web of love by reaching across the circle and holding the wrists of two people.**

Pause while kids respond, then say: **Lying, stealing, and killing tangle us up in bad ways. When we follow God's commandments, we create a web of love with God and with one another. We are all special people. We please God with our actions.**

the POINT

Close with a prayer. Then, one at a time, have kids say, "God loves us, so we love each other." Then have them lightly squeeze the wrists they are holding. Continue around the circle until everyone has had a turn.

As kids let go of wrists and untangle the web of love, remind them to follow God's commandments this next week and act in ways that are pleasing to him.

LESSON 8:
GOD-PLEASING ACTIONS

the POINT **We please God with our actions.**

Hands-On FUN AT HOME

BIBLE FOCUS

"Love the Lord your God with all your heart, all your soul, and all your strength" (Deuteronomy 6:5).

LAUGH it UP

I'M SURE THERE'S ONE KIND OF LYING THAT'S OK WITH GOD.
YEAH? WHAT?
WHEN I LIE DOWN TO GO TO SLEEP!

FAITH walk

Play this guessing game with your family this week. Each night, a different person picks an event from Jesus' life that pleased God, then gives clues to the rest of the family. Examples of a time that Jesus pleased God are when Jesus healed a blind man (Mark 8:22-25) and when Jesus was baptized (Matthew 3:13-17). After you've guessed the pleasing action, read about it together in the Bible.

WAY to PRAY

Praise is an action that is pleasing to God! Gather your whole family together and read Psalm 71:5-6. Then, on a sheet of paper, list things you want to praise and thank God for, such as family members, forgiveness, love, home, food, and health. Read your praises together each night before you go to bed!

CHECK it OUT

Read Psalm 25:4-5.
Think of a time when you told the truth even though it was difficult. How did telling the truth help you feel close to God?

Read John 8:31-32.
How do lies keep you from being free? How does telling the truth make you free?

Read Psalm 119:1-3.
Tell about some times you have been happy because you have lived according to God's rules.

LESSON 9

DON'T EVEN THINK IT!

THE POINT

We please God with our thoughts.

THE BIBLE BASIS

Exodus 20:17. Don't covet.

God knows that thoughts come before actions. Theft, lies, murder—all these actions begin with a person's thoughts. When Jesus interpreted the commandments, he explained that anger is like murdering a person in one's heart. God wants our thoughts, as well as our actions, to be free from evil intentions. Love and bitter feelings simply aren't compatible.

Third- and fourth-graders know what it means to want what someone else has. Coveting can cause many problems, such as jealousy, hatred, low self-esteem, theft, lying, and so on. You can help your third- and fourth-graders recognize that wishful thinking is often the beginning of discontent and violence. Use this lesson to help kids recognize that in order to live in harmony with God and others, we need to focus on being thankful for what we have—not jealous of the possessions of others.

Other Scriptures used in this lesson are **Exodus 20:17; Psalm 139:1-2, 13-14, 23-24; Matthew 5:21-22; 15:18-19;** and **Philippians 4:8-9.**

GETTING THE POINT

Students will

- play a game in which "thoughts" are similar to murder,
- learn that Jesus compared anger to murder,
- compare how we look or talk to how we think or feel, and
- choose to think appropriate thoughts.

THIS LESSON AT A GLANCE

Before the lesson, collect the necessary items from the Learning Lab for the activities you plan to use. Refer to the pictures in the margin to see what each item looks like.

SECTION	MINUTES	WHAT STUDENTS WILL DO	LEARNING LAB SUPPLIES	CLASSROOM SUPPLIES
ATTENTION GRABBER	up to 10	**MURDER!**—Play a game where thinking is like murder.	Plastic egg	Bibles, paper slips, pencil
BIBLE EXPLORATION AND APPLICATION	up to 15	**WISHFUL THINKING**—Listen to a unique conversation on the cassette tape and read Exodus 20:17; Matthew 15:18-19; and Philippians 4:8-9.	Cassette: "I Only Thought It"	Bibles, cassette player
	up to 15	**SHINING GOOD ACTIONS**—Read Philippians 4:8-9 and brainstorm good actions that might come from good thoughts.	Prism shapes	Bibles, newsprint, tape, markers
	up to 15	**WHO SHOULD KNOW?**—Discuss private thoughts and read Psalm 139:1-2, 23-24.	Neon kite string	Bibles
CLOSING	up to 5	**HAPPY TO BE ME**—Hear Psalm 139:13-14, and affirm that they are happy to be the people God created them to be.		Bibles, paper, pencils

Remember to make photocopies of the "Hands-On Fun at Home" handout (p. 119) to send home with your kids. The "Fun at Home" handout suggests ways for kids to talk with their families about what they're learning in class and helps them put their faith into action.

THE LESSON

LEARNING LAB

As kids arrive, ask them which "Fun at Home" activities they tried. Ask questions such as "What things did your family praise God for?" and "What pleasing actions from Jesus' life did you read about with your family?"

Tell kids that whenever you blow the *trumpet* twice, they are to stop talking, raise their hands, and focus on you. Explain that it's important to respond to this signal quickly so the class can do as many fun activities as possible.

MODULE REVIEW

Use the casual interaction time at the beginning of the class to ask kids the following module-review questions.

- **In what creative ways have you worshiped God during the past few weeks?**
- **In what restful ways did you remember the Lord's day?**
- **What nice things have you done for your family members recently?**
- **What's your favorite thing we've learned during the past few weeks? Why?**
- **How is your life different as a result of what we've learned during the past five weeks?**

ATTENTION GRABBER

MURDER!
(up to 10 minutes)

LEARNING LAB

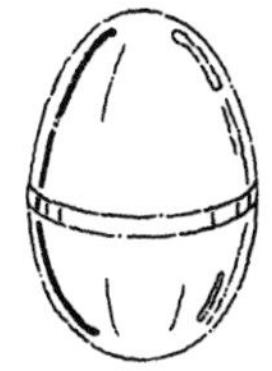

You'll need one slip of paper for each person in your class. Mark an X on two of the slips of paper. Fold all the slips, and place them in a *plastic egg*.

Gather the kids in a circle. Say: **We're going to play a game called Murder. I'll pass around this *plastic egg* filled with slips of paper. Two of the slips are marked with an X. The rest of the slips are blank. Don't let anyone see your slip of paper. If you get an X, you're the "murderer" and can wink at others to "kill" them. If you get a blank paper slip, you can be killed when the murderer winks at you. Nobody should say anything during the game. Just look quietly around the circle. If somebody winks at you, wait five seconds, then lie down to show you're dead.**

After several kids have gotten killed, blow the *trumpet* twice, and wait for kids to respond. If you have time, gather the paper slips in the *plastic egg*, and play the game again. Ask:

- **What was it like to pretend to kill others during this game?** (It

> **TEACHER TIP**
>
> If there are fewer than 10 students in your class, choose only one person to be the "murderer."

was fun; it was hard to do it so nobody would know I was the killer.)

● **How did the rest of you feel as you looked around the circle of potential killers?** (I kept wondering who the murderers were; I kept wondering if I would get killed next; I kept hoping I wouldn't have to get killed.)

● **What would it be like if killing were this easy in real life?** (It would be terrible; awful; scary.)

● **Why would it be so bad?** (Because anybody could kill you just by looking at you; you could get killed by someone who even thought about killing you; I'd be scared all the time.)

Say: **We can't kill with our thoughts, but our thoughts are still very powerful. Let's find out more.** Distribute Bibles and help kids find **Matthew 5:21-22.** Have a volunteer read the passage aloud while others follow along in their Bibles. Ask:

● **What were the two things in this verse that Jesus said we will be judged for?** (Anger and murder; being mad at your brother and killing him.)

● **How are anger and murder alike?** (Sometimes you're so mad that you want to kill someone; when you feel angry, you may wish someone were dead.)

the POINT

Say: **During our game, we winked at each other to commit murder. I'm glad none of you could really get killed! But Jesus tells us that what we think has a big effect on how we act. Evil actions come from evil thoughts. Good actions come from good thoughts. When we have the right kinds of thoughts, we act right, and we please God with our thoughts.**

Collect the *plastic egg,* and place it out of sight for use in future lessons.

BIBLE EXPLORATION AND APPLICATION

LEARNING LAB

WISHFUL THINKING
(up to 15 minutes)

Say: **Sometimes our thoughts can lead to harmful actions. I'll play a conversation for you. One voice represents what the person actually says. The other voice represents what the person is thinking.**

Play "I Only Thought It" on the *cassette tape.* Then ask the kids to stand.

Say: **Raise your hands when you've thought of an answer to each of the questions I'm about to ask. I'd like to hear lots of different, interesting answers. When someone gives an answer you've thought of and you don't have anything more to add, you may sit down. When everyone is seated, I'll ask you to stand again for the next question.** Ask:

● **What feelings did you have as you listened to this tape?** (It made me feel bad for the other kid; it was kind of scary; I wondered if lots of people think things like that.)

● **What was the person on the tape doing?** (The person was saying one thing and thinking something else; the person seemed to be a friend but really wasn't; the person wanted things that belonged to the other person.)

● **How do you think the person on the tape felt?** (Jealous; unhappy; sad.)

● **How is what you heard on the tape like what can happen in real life?** (People often want what other people have; kids feel bad when their things aren't as good as somebody else's.)

Say: **Let's see what the Bible says about wishing for things that belong to other people.**

Form pairs and help kids find **Exodus 20:17** in their Bibles. Have a volunteer read the verse aloud as others follow along in their own Bibles. Then help kids find **Matthew 15:18-19.** Have partners each read a verse aloud.

After partners have finished reading the verses, have them discuss the following questions. Pause after you ask each question to allow time for discussion. Ask:

● **What is God telling us in these verses?** (That it's wrong to want what belongs to someone else; that we should control what we wish for; that God doesn't want us to even think about taking someone else's stuff.)

● **Why do you think God cares about what we think?** (Wanting what belongs to your friend can ruin your friendship; wishing for more things makes you unhappy with what you have; you could start to hate other people because they have more things than you do.)

● **If people did what they were thinking, what could happen?** (They might steal or lie; they could hurt someone; somebody could get killed.)

● **When have you done something wrong because of what you were thinking?** (When I hit my brother because I was mad; when I broke my friend's game because I didn't want her to have one.)

● **When have you done something good because of what you were thinking?** (When I did something special for my sister because she was feeling unhappy; when we gave food to the homeless.)

Blow the *trumpet* twice, and wait for kids to respond. Invite them to share insights from their discussions.

Say: **Thinking wrong thoughts can lead to wrong actions. God likes our thoughts to be about things that are good and right. We please God with our thoughts. Let's look at another Bible verse that tells more about the ways people think and the actions that come from their thoughts.**

TEACHER TIP

Encourage active participation in the discussion by following up kids' answers with questions such as "What did you mean by that?" and "Can you tell me more?"

TEACHER TIP

It's important to say The Point just as it's written in each activity. Repeating The Point over and over will help kids remember it and apply it to their lives.

the POINT

LEARNING LAB

SHINING GOOD ACTIONS
(up to 15 minutes)

Help kids find **Philippians 4:8-9,** then ask a volunteer to read the passage aloud. Ask:

- **What do you think happens when people follow this advice?** (They are happy; people like them; they have a good life from God.)
- **What are some thoughts that God would consider good and right?** (Love for your family; kind thoughts about your friends; ideas to do good deeds for others.)

Say: **Let's brainstorm good actions that come from good thoughts.**

Form no more than four groups. Say: **Quickly choose a recorder to write down your ideas, an encourager to urge people to contribute to your discussion, and a reporter to read your ideas to the class.**

> **TEACHER TIP**
>
> If you have more than three students in each group, have more than one student be an encourager.

While kids are assigning roles, give each group a sheet of newsprint, a marker, a strip of masking tape, and five *prism shapes.* Then say: **Brainstorm "shining good actions" that come from good thoughts, such as giving blankets to the homeless or bringing canned goods to share with poor families. Recorders, write your groups' ideas on your newsprint. Tape a *prism shape* next to each shining good action. Try to think of at least five good actions.**

> **TEACHER TIP**
>
> If kids have trouble thinking of shining good actions, suggest ideas such as writing a thank you note, taking out the garbage without being told, or helping a younger brother or sister with homework.

After five minutes, blow the *trumpet* twice, and wait for kids to respond. Ask reporters to read their groups' shining good actions. Tape the sheets of newsprint to a wall.

After all ideas are reported, say: **God knows that our thoughts are important because good thoughts lead to good actions. When we think in loving ways toward others, we please God with our thoughts.**

the POINT

Leave the sheets of newsprint taped to the wall throughout the lesson.

LEARNING LAB

WHO SHOULD KNOW?
(up to 15 minutes)

Say: **When you think or do something you're ashamed of, you probably don't want many people to know about it. When you think or do something great, you probably want lots of people to know. Let's play a game to find out what you might or might not want people to know.**

Form a large circle on the floor with the *neon kite string.* Have everyone stand outside the circle.

Say: **I'm going to ask some questions. If your answer is "yes," step inside the circle. If your answer is "no," step outside the circle.**

Pause after you ask each question. Allow kids time to discuss their responses with others close by. Prompt discussion with questions such as "When has something like this ever happened to you?" and "What do you think would happen if you shared what you were thinking?" Ask:

● **Would you tell your mother what you're thinking of buying her for her birthday?**

● **Would you want your teacher to know that you were daydreaming and didn't hear half the words he read?**

● **Would you want your brother to know that you think his hair is too long and that he needs a haircut?**

● **If your dad bought tickets for a play and you'd rather go to a ballgame, would you tell him?**

● **Would you tell your best friend that you're jealous of her because she always gets good grades?**

● **Would you tell your parents that the idea you thought of for school safety week was voted best in the class?**

Have kids sit in a circle around the *neon kite string*. Ask:

● **What's it like when somebody finds out you've thought or done something that you're proud of?** (I'm happy; people tell me they're proud of me; I feel glad.)

● **What's it like when somebody finds out that you've thought or done something that you're not proud of?** (I'm embarrassed; I wish it hadn't happened; I try to do better the next time.)

Place the *neon kite string* out of sight for use in future lessons.

Say: **We may be able to keep our thoughts hidden from other people, but we can't hide our thoughts from God. Let's look at a Bible verse about God and our thoughts.**

Help kids find **Psalm 139:1-2** in their Bibles. Ask a volunteer to read the passage aloud as the others follow along in their own Bibles. Ask:

● **What is your reaction to God knowing your thoughts?** (OK, because I can pray silently in my mind and know God still hears me; it's not so good because God probably doesn't like all my thoughts.)

● **What can you do about your not-so-good thoughts?** (Think about something else; tell God I'm sorry; think good thoughts instead.)

Say: **When we have the wrong kinds of thoughts, it's important to ask God to forgive us. One person wrote a prayer about this. Let's look up that prayer and use it for our prayer.**

Help kids find **Psalm 139:23-24.** Read the verses together as a prayer.

Say: **God knows all about us, and he knows what we're thinking. God wants our thoughts to be good. We please God with our thoughts.**

the POINT

Hands-On FUN AT HOME

We believe that Christian education extends beyond the classroom into the home. Photocopy the "Hands-On Fun at Home" handout (p. 119) for this week, and send it home with your kids. Encourage kids to try several activities and discuss the Bible verses and questions with their parents.

CLOSING

HAPPY TO BE ME
(up to 5 minutes)

Say: **Today we've discussed our thoughts and how good thoughts lead to good actions. Now let's think about thoughts we have about ourselves. Sometimes we want to be someone else because we think that person is more talented than we are or has a better life than we do. It's easy to compare ourselves to others and feel jealous. And it's easy to get mad at ourselves when we think we can't do things as well as others.**

Give each person a sheet of paper and a pencil. Say: **Think about the negative messages you tell yourself; for example, "I'm no good at sports." Write a few negative messages on your paper.**

After one minute, ask:

- **Why do we think negative thoughts about ourselves?** (We get jealous; we are too hard on ourselves; we compare ourselves to others.)
- **How do you think God wants us to think about ourselves?** (God wants us to be happy; God wants us to like ourselves; God doesn't want us to compare.)

Say: **We can turn to Psalms to find out more.** Read **Psalm 139:13-14.** Then ask:

- **According to these verses, what does God think about us?** (He created us and loves us; we are amazing and wonderful; God knows all about us.)

Say: **Now, turn your paper over and write a few positive messages about yourself; for example, "God made me in an amazing and wonderful way."**

the POINT

After a minute, say: **God made each person here. He knows all about us—even our thoughts. God wants us to think good thoughts and follow his commandments. We're happy when we please God with our thoughts.**

Close with a prayer thanking God for creating each wonderful student in your class.

JOSHUA

Heroes. They loom larger than life on every TV screen in every child's home. Athletes, musicians, cartoon characters, TV and movie stars—never have kids had so many choices for heroes. And never has the list lacked more in godliness and high moral character. When we look to the media or to public life, it's not easy to find role models we'd be comfortable having our students follow. Fortunately, we can also look to God's Word.

In this module your kids will meet a Bible hero whose life shines with courage, faith, integrity, and unshakable faith in God. Joshua goes from one breathtaking adventure to another, conquering God's enemies at every step. As kids study Joshua's life, they'll learn to make wise judgments about what makes a hero. And they'll be challenged to take a stand for God, just as Joshua did.

JOSHUA

LESSON	PAGE	THE POINT	THE BIBLE BASIS
10—STAND FIRM!	125	True heroes stand up for what they believe.	Numbers 13:1–14:30
11—TRUST GOD!	137	True heroes trust in God.	Joshua 1:1-9
12—GOING GOD'S WAY	147	True heroes follow God's directions.	Joshua 3:1–4:24
13—SHOW THEM THE WAY	159	True heroes encourage others to follow God.	Joshua 2:1-21; 6:1-27

THE SIGNAL

LEARNING LAB

During the lessons on Joshua, your attention-getting signal will be to sound the *trumpet* found in the Learning Lab. Blow the *trumpet* twice whenever you want to get kids back together. In response to the two horn blasts, kids should immediately stop talking, raise their hands, and focus their attention on you.

Tell kids about this signal—and practice it—before starting each lesson. Explain that it's important to respond to this signal quickly so the class can do as many fun activities as possible. During the lessons, you'll be prompted when to use the signal.

LEARNING LAB

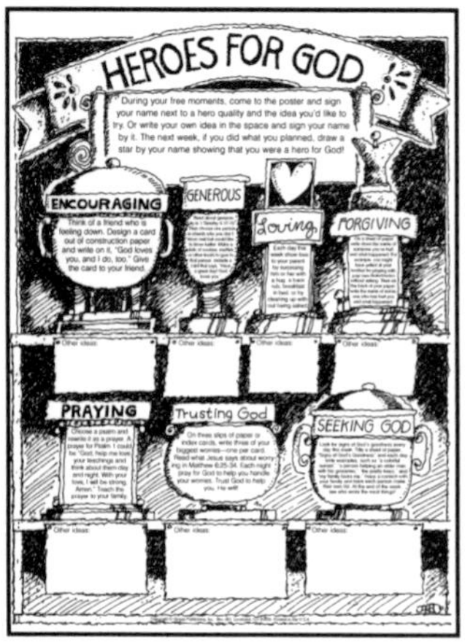

THE TIME STUFFER

This module's Time Stuffer is the "Heroes for God" poster found in the Learning Lab. Each trophy in the trophy case shows one quality of a hero and one way kids can practice that quality and be a hero during the next week. The trophies also contain space for kids to write their own ways to be heroes. During their free moments, kids can go to the poster and sign their names next to the ideas they'd like to try. Or they can write ideas of their own. The next week kids can draw stars by their names, showing that they were heroes for God!

At the end of the month, you'll have a class full of heroes for God and a trophy case to prove it!

REMEMBERING THE BIBLE

Each four- or five-week module focuses on a key Bible verse. The key verse for this module is "Be strong and brave. Don't be afraid, because the Lord your God will be with you everywhere you go" **(Joshua 1:9).**

The following are two activities you may do with your third- and fourth-graders to help them remember this Bible verse and apply it to their lives.

LEARNING LAB

PRISM POWER

Form three teams. Give a *prism shape* to each person in team 1. Tell the kids on team 2 they are "It." Tell the kids on team 3 they'll be chased by team 2. Say: **We're going to play Tag. Team 3, if you are tagged, you have to sit down. Team 1, if you're holding a *prism shape,* that means you're safe—no one can tag you! In fact, if kids on team 2 try to tag you, they have to sit down. But holding the *prism shape* also means you have to help the people on team 3 who are tagged by pulling them back to their feet. When a person is pulled up, he or she is in the game again. Ready? Play Tag!**

Play for two minutes, then blow the *trumpet* twice, and wait for kids to respond. Switch team roles. When all teams have had a chance to hold the *prism shapes,* collect the *prism shapes,* and have kids form a large circle. Ask:

- **How did you feel when you were holding the *prism shape?*** (Special; safe; like no one could get me.)
- **How did you feel without the *prism shape?*** (Scared; like anyone could tag me; tired.)

Distribute Bibles, and help kids find **Joshua 1:9.** Ask a volunteer to read the verse aloud. Then have kids repeat the verse with you. Ask:

- **How were the *prism shapes* in this game like God's presence?**

(Having the *prism shape* was like having God protect me; I was safe when I had the *prism shape,* and I'm safe with God.)

● **In our game, people with *prism shapes* helped others stand up. How can you use God's strength to help others?** (I can help them when others tease them; I can stand by them and be their friend; I can help them stand up for what's right.)

Say: **We can be strong and brave, just like Joshua. We can stand strong for God, because everywhere we go, God will be with us. Let's say the verse together again.** Lead kids in repeating the key verse. **Remember to stand strong for God this week, and help your friends stand strong, too.**

BE BRAVE!

Have kids sit in a circle, then turn off the lights. Say: **Think of what scares you the most, such as a storm or a stranger breaking into your house. Whisper what scares you to the people on both sides of you.**

Give kids a few moments to share, then blow the *trumpet* twice, and wait for kids to respond. Ask:

● **Why do these things scare you?** (I'm afraid of the unknown; I wouldn't know what to do; I don't want to get hurt.)

● **What makes you feel better when you're scared?** (Having the lights turned on; being with my parents; being with a friend.)

Turn on the lights and distribute Bibles. Help kids find **Joshua 1:9.** Have a volunteer read the verse aloud while everyone else follows along. Print the verse on a chalkboard or on newsprint. Ask:

● **How can this verse help you the next time you feel scared?** (I'll know God is with me no matter where I am; God loves me and doesn't want me to be scared; God wants me to be brave.)

● **What is it like to know that God is with you always?** (Comforting; wonderful; nice; safe.)

Then have everyone read the verse from the chalkboard with the lights on!

LESSON 10

STAND FIRM!

THE POINT

True heroes stand up for what they believe.

THE BIBLE BASIS

Numbers 13:1–14:30. The 12 spies go into Canaan.

The Israelites escaped from Egypt, persevered in the desert, and found themselves within reach of Canaan—the Promised Land! Moses sent 12 spies to scout the land. Ten spies reported, "We can't attack these people; they are stronger than we are." Only Joshua and Caleb stood firm and said, "Don't be afraid of the people in that land! We will chew them up. They have no protection, but the Lord is with us. So don't be afraid of them!" The people listened to the 10 and wanted to kill Joshua and Caleb. But God intervened. He punished the people by refusing to let them ever see the Promised Land. Only Joshua and Caleb could enter the land because they stood firm in their faith in God.

Third- and fourth-graders are often called on to stand up for their beliefs. Kids face constant pressure to cheat, disobey, swear, lie, and misbehave. Walking away from those pressures isn't always easy. Use this lesson to help kids learn how to stand up for what they believe—no matter what others do or say. Help your students see that because God is with them, they don't have to be afraid!

Other Scriptures used in this lesson are **Joshua 1:9** and **1 Corinthians 15:58; 16:13.**

GETTING THE POINT

Students will

- explore what it means to be heroes,
- stand up for their beliefs,
- help one another stand firm, and
- pray for the strength to stand firm in daily life.

THIS LESSON AT A GLANCE

Before the lesson, collect the necessary items from the Learning Lab for the activities you plan to use. Refer to the pictures in the margin to see what each item looks like.

SECTION	MINUTES	WHAT STUDENTS WILL DO	LEARNING LAB SUPPLIES	CLASSROOM SUPPLIES
ATTENTION GRABBER	up to 10	**WHO'S A HERO?**—Race to name their heroes.	Trumpets	Tape, newsprint, markers
BIBLE EXPLORATION AND APPLICATION	up to 15	**SPY ASSIGNMENT**—Search for clues and listen to the Canaan spy story from Numbers 13:1–14:30.	Cassette: "Spy Assignment" and "Canaan Vote," spy disguise, wall walker	Bibles, cassette player, paper slips, pencil
	up to 15	**RINGING A HERO**—Play a game about heroes and read 1 Corinthians 15:58.	Colored rings	Bibles
	up to 15	**FIRM IN THE FAITH**—Stand strong in specific situations and read 1 Corinthians 16:13-14.	Gift box, miniature trophy, catch ball ring, tool kit	Bibles, pencils, "Stand-Strong Skits" handout (p. 134), scissors
CLOSING	up to 5	**HERO HAUL**—Read Joshua 1:9, then help each other stand up for what they believe.	Terry rope	Bible

Hands-On FUN AT HOME

Remember to make photocopies of the "Hands-On Fun at Home" handout (p. 135) to send home with your kids. The "Fun at Home" handout suggests ways for kids to talk with their families about what they're learning in class and helps them put their faith into action.

THE LESSON

LEARNING LAB

As kids arrive, ask them which "Fun at Home" activities they tried. Ask questions such as "What good thoughts about each other did your family members share?" and "How did God help you think good thoughts last week?"

Tell kids that whenever you blow the *trumpet* twice, they are to stop talking, raise their hands, and focus on you. Explain that it's important to respond to this signal quickly so the class can do as many fun activities as possible.

ATTENTION GRABBER

WHO'S A HERO?
(up to 10 minutes)

LEARNING LAB

Tape two sheets of newsprint to a wall. Place a marker beneath each sheet. Form two teams, and have them line up on the side of the room opposite the newsprint. Give the first person in each line a *trumpet.*

Say: **Today we're going to talk about heroes. But first we're going to have a race. When I say, "Name your heroes," the first person in each line passes the *trumpet* overhead to the person behind, who grabs it and passes it underneath his or her legs to the next person behind, and so on. Continue passing over and under until the last person in line has the *trumpet.* Then that person runs to the newsprint and writes the name of a hero. It can be someone in your family; a teacher; a movie or sports star; or a cartoon, TV, or movie character.**

After you've written the name of your hero, run to the front of your line and hand the *trumpet* overhead to the person behind. Pass the *trumpet* over and under again, and continue until everyone has written the name of a hero on your newsprint. Each person on the team needs to write a different hero's name. Let's see who can finish first. Ready? Name your heroes!

When both teams have finished, have them applaud one another's efforts. Then have everyone find a partner from the opposite team and sit down. Collect the *trumpets.*

Have partners each identify the hero they named on the newsprint. Then have partners discuss the following questions. Pause after you ask each question to allow time for discussion. Ask:

- **What qualities do you admire about your hero?** (He's a great athlete; she's a talented and famous singer; he's rich.)
- **Could your hero do anything that would make you stop admiring him or her? Explain.** (No, I like the person just as he is; yes, if he did drugs I wouldn't like him anymore; yes, if she lives a wild life.)
- **What does your hero's behavior tell you about his or her**

> **TEACHER TIP**
>
> Be sure to wash the *trumpets* in warm, soapy water so they are ready for other kids to use in future lessons.

TEACHER TIP

It's important to say The Point just as it's written in each activity. Repeating The Point over and over will help kids remember it and apply it to their lives.

beliefs? (He's against doing drugs because he talks to schools about it; she believes in God because her songs are about Jesus; he believes money and possessions are important because he always has the best of everything.)

● **What do you think God looks for in a hero?** (Someone who's not afraid; someone who'll help people and stick up for what's right.)

● **What do you think God would think about the heroes on our lists?** (Some of them aren't very good heroes; God would want us to have better heroes; he'd like them.)

Blow the *trumpet* twice to bring everyone together. Wait for kids to respond, then invite them to share insights from their discussions.

the POINT

Say: **Sometimes the people who we think are heroes turn out not to be heroes at all. True heroes stand up for what they believe. And that can be really hard sometimes. Today we're going to see why it's so important to stand up for our beliefs and how we can help each other stand strong.**

BIBLE EXPLORATION AND APPLICATION

SPY ASSIGNMENT
(up to 15 minutes)

LEARNING LAB

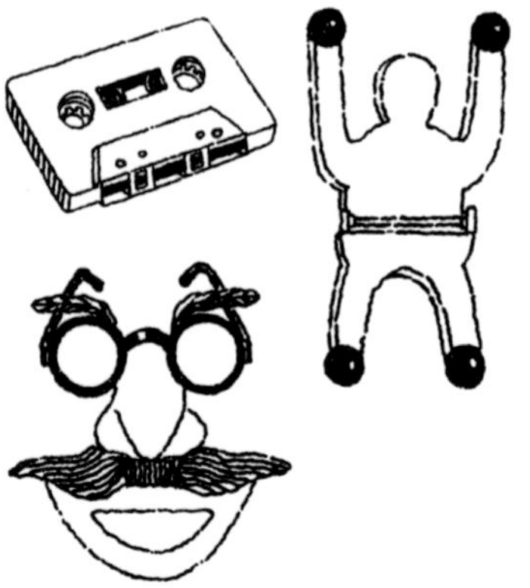

Before class, copy the following clues onto slips of paper. If you have more than 10 students in your class, you'll need to copy additional clues so each student will have one. Hide the clues around your classroom.

- The people look like giants.
- The land flows with milk and honey.
- The cities are enormous!
- The people are stronger than we are.
- The land looks wonderful!
- The people are too tall.
- We can easily take the land ourselves.
- The land is too large to conquer.
- The Lord will lead us into the land.
- We look like grasshoppers compared to the people in the land.

Distribute Bibles and help kids find **Numbers 13:1-25.** Say: **Today our Bible story involves heroes from the book of Numbers. We're going to listen to the first part of a story about some heroes named Joshua and Caleb. These heroes were sent with 10 other spies on a dangerous mission. Let's listen to the story and discover what happened to our heroes.**

Play the "Spy Assignment" section of the *cassette tape*.

Stop the *cassette tape* and say: **Now we get to take turns spying on the land of Canaan and bringing back clues. After we hear our spies' reports, we'll vote on whether the land is safe to enter.**

TEACHER TIP

The *wall walker* works best on a smooth surface. If your classroom walls are rough, carefully use the *wall walker* on glass, such as a window or mirror.

Bring out the *spy disguise* and the *wall walker.*

Give the *spy disguise* to the person sitting closest to you, and have him or her put it on. Say: **This person is the first spy we'll send into Canaan. This *wall walker* is the timer. I've hidden several slips of paper that contain clues about Canaan. I'll place the *wall walker* as high up on a wall as I can reach. When I let go, the spy will search the room for a clue. The spy has until the *wall walker* reaches the floor to find a clue. When a clue is found, the spy holds on to it and hands the *spy disguise* to another person. Then the first spy places the *wall walker* as high up on a wall as possible, then the second spy searches for a clue. If the *wall walker* gets close to the ground before a spy finds a clue, I'll give hints about where to search.**

After everyone has had a turn searching for a clue, have kids sit in a circle. Put the *spy disguise* and *wall walker* away for use in future lessons.

One at a time, ask kids to read aloud their clues. Then say: **According to the clues, raise your hand if you think we should enter the land of Canaan.** Count the votes, then ask:

- **What Canaan clues made you vote the way you did?** (I didn't want to go to Canaan because I'm scared of giants; I wanted to go to Canaan because it's a rich land.)
- **How do you feel about your decision?** (Good; happy; unsure; bad.)

Help kids find **Numbers 13:25.** Have a volunteer read the verse aloud. Say: **Let's find out what happened when the spies returned with their reports. Listen to the rest of our story on the *cassette tape.* Let's hear the Israelites vote on whether or not to enter Canaan.**

Then play the "Canaan Vote" segment of the *cassette tape.*

When the cassette segment ends, have the kids stand up. Say: **Raise your hand when you've thought of an answer to each of the questions I'm about to ask. I'd like to hear lots of different, interesting answers. When someone gives an answer you've thought of and you don't have anything more to add, you may sit down. When everyone is seated, I'll ask you to stand again for the next question.** Ask:

- **How do you think Joshua and Caleb felt as they stood up for what they believed?** (Happy that they trusted God; sorry for the people; mad at the people for not listening to them; scared because the people wanted to stone them.)
- **When do you stand up for what you believe?** (When my friends do things I know are wrong; when a new kid at school is picked on.)
- **How do you feel in those situations?** (Scared; proud; nervous about what my friends will say.)
- **What helps you stand up for what you know is right?** (Praying; talking to my parents; getting away and thinking about what's right.)
- **Why were Joshua and Caleb heroes?** (Because they stood up for their beliefs; because they listened to God; they weren't afraid.)

Say: **When we have to stand up for our beliefs, it helps to**

TEACHER TIP

For a large class, send kids out in pairs to search for clues. Give one partner the *spy disguise* to wear and the other partner a *terry rope* to tie around his or her forehead.

remember God's promises. Then we can stand firm without any doubt! Joshua and Caleb may have been afraid of the Canaanites, but they also believed God's promise to help them conquer the land. **True heroes stand up for what they believe. Let's play a game to learn more about standing up for what we believe.**

the POINT

LEARNING LAB

RINGING A HERO
(up to 15 minutes)

Form three groups. Say: **Group 1, you're the Outstanding Heroes. Scatter throughout the room, and stand still for the entire game. Group 2, you're the Hero Protectors. Your job is to stand in front of the Outstanding Heroes and protect them from group 3. Group 3, you're the Hero Ringers.** Give each Hero Ringer several *colored rings.* **Your job is to try to get past the Hero Protectors and throw your *colored rings* at the Outstanding Heroes. If you hit an Outstanding Hero with a *colored ring,* the hero and his or her protector must sit down. Hero Ringers, when you have thrown all your rings, you must sit down. Ready? Ring a hero!**

Continue the game until all the Outstanding Heroes are sitting down (or for no longer than five minutes). Blow the *trumpet* twice, and wait for kids to respond. Collect the *colored rings,* and put them away for use in future lessons. Then form trios with one Outstanding Hero, one Hero Protector, and one Hero Ringer in each trio. Pause after you ask each of the following questions to allow time for discussion. Ask:

- **What was it like to be an Outstanding Hero?** (Scary; fun; it made me nervous; OK.)
- **What was it like to be a Hero Protector?** (Good; I felt like I was helping someone; fun; I felt important.)
- **What was it like to be a Hero Ringer?** (Fun; I felt mean; it was hard to get around the Hero Protectors.)
- **How was this activity like what happens in real life when you stand up for what you believe?** (It's hard to stand up for what I believe when I get attacked; I can protect my friends and help them stand up for what they believe.)
- **Which group in our game do you feel most like in real life? Explain.** (An Outstanding Hero, because I feel nervous when I have to stand up for my beliefs; a Hero Protector, because I like to help my friends stand up for what's right.)

Blow the *trumpet* twice to bring everyone together. Wait for kids to respond, then invite them to share the insights they discovered in their discussions.

Say: **Standing up for what you believe can be scary. In the game, you may have felt like a target. In real life, you can stand firm, and you can help your friends stand firm. Let's read what the Bible says about this.**

Help kids find **1 Corinthians 15:58** in their Bibles. Have a volunteer read the verse aloud. Then ask:

● **What does it mean to stand firm?** (Doing what's right; following God; standing up for our beliefs; being strong Christians.)

● **How can you help others stand firm?** (Pray for them; encourage them; stand up to others with them; protect them from people who want to lead them the wrong way.)

● **What happens when we help each other stand firm?** (We all get stronger; it's easier to make the right choices and stand up for what we believe; we feel better.)

Say: **True heroes stand up for what they believe, and that makes it easier for others to do the same. When everyone stands strong, we can accomplish great things for God!**

the POINT

FIRM IN THE FAITH
(up to 15 minutes)

LEARNING LAB

Photocopy the "Stand-Strong Skits" handout (p. 134), and cut apart the cards. Form four groups, and give each group a pencil, a card from the handout, and the corresponding item from the Learning Lab box.

Say: **You'll have five minutes to read your situation, then discuss it and write on the back of your card how you'll stand firm in your situation. Prepare your "Stand-Strong Skit" to present to the rest of the class. Choose a reader to read your situation to the class. Then choose two people to act out the roles. The rest of your group will help brainstorm and direct your skit.**

Allow five minutes for kids to prepare their skits, then blow the *trumpet* twice, and wait for kids to respond. Gather kids in a semicircle, and have groups take turns performing their skits. After each skit, have everyone clap and say, "Way to stand firm!"

After the performances, place the Learning Lab items out of sight for use in future lessons. Ask:

● **How were the people in your skits like the people in today's Bible story?** (The characters weren't afraid to stand up for what's right; some people did what God wanted them to do, and some people didn't.)

● **Have you ever experienced situations like these in real life? What happened?** (A friend wanted me to steal candy from a store; lots of kids like to tease new people at school; I saw someone cheat on a test.)

● **How did you respond in those situations?** (I got scared; I felt bad, but I didn't say anything; I stood up for what was right.)

● **Why is it hard to stand up for what you believe?** (My friends might think I'm weird; I don't know what to say; people make fun of me.)

Say: **The Bible encourages us to be strong. Let's look at this next verse together.** Help kids find **1 Corinthians 16:13** in their Bibles. Have a volunteer read the verse aloud. Then ask:

● **How does that verse make you feel about standing strong?** (Strong; good; excited; like I could stand firm; wonderful.)

TEACHER TIP
If your class really enjoys drama and acting, consider doing this activity in pairs so all the kids get a chance to act. It's OK to give the same situation to more than one group.

the POINT

Say: **Turn to a partner, and tell him or her one way you can be strong this week. For example, you might say, "I can be kind to new kids when my friends are mean," "I can invite a friend to church," or "I can be nice to my sister when she picks on me."**

Have kids stand in a circle. Say: **True heroes stand up for what they believe. We can be heroes for God by standing strong in our faith, just as Joshua and Caleb did. Let's read 1 Corinthians 16:13 again, but this time we'll all read it together *loudly!* The first time we say "strong," we'll flex the muscles in our right arms. I'll start first, and we'll continue around the circle—like a wave.** Practice the motion. **The second time we say "strong," we'll flex the muscles in our left arms. I'll start first, and we'll continue around the circle in the opposite direction.** Practice the motion.

Read the verse loudly and do the actions.

> **Hands-On FUN AT HOME**
>
> We believe that Christian education extends beyond the classroom into the home. Photocopy the "Hands-On Fun at Home" handout (p. 135) for this week, and send it home with your kids. Encourage kids to try several activities and discuss the Bible verses and questions with their parents.

CLOSING

LEARNING LAB

HERO HAUL
(up to 5 minutes)

Ask:

- **What have we discovered today about what makes a person a hero?** (It's someone who stands up for what's right; true heroes stand up for what they believe; heroes follow God no matter what.)

Say: **Let's read one more verse to help us remember what we've learned.** Read **Joshua 1:9.** Then have kids scatter throughout the room and sit down.

Bring out a *terry rope,* then say: **I'll hand one end of this *terry rope* to someone and affirm him or her by saying,** "(Name), **God is with you. Stand up for what you believe." Then I'll pull that person up from the floor and give him or her the *terry rope.* I'll stand behind that person, hold on to his or her shoulders, and we'll go to another person in the room and do the same thing. We'll continue until we form one long line and we pull everyone up.**

the POINT

When the last person has been affirmed and pulled up, put the *terry rope* away, and gather everyone in a circle. Say: **True heroes stand up for what they believe. And when we help each other stand**

strong in faith, we're all heroes for God!

Close in prayer, asking God for strength to stand firm this week and thanking him for this class full of heroes.

STAND-STRONG SKITS

Gift-Box Grab

Allison and Patti are shopping at the mall. Allison holds the *gift box* and tells Patti to slip it in her pocket and walk out of the store without paying for it.

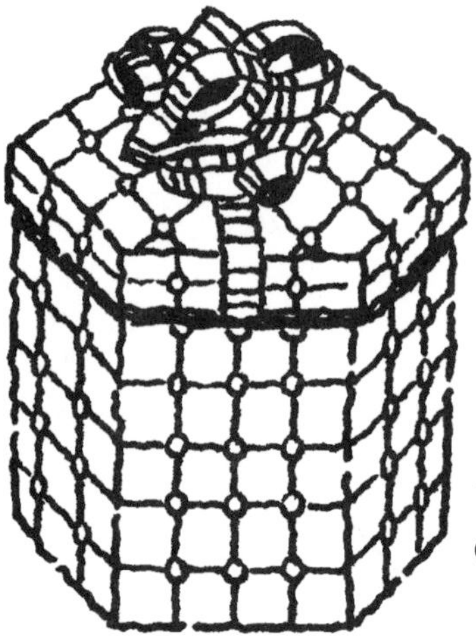

Decide how Patti can stand firm in this situation. Then choose two people to act out the situation and Patti's response for the rest of the class.

Catch-Ball-Ring Keepaway

Fred wears the *catch ball ring* and tosses the ball up and down. Fred tells David, "Help me play a trick on a new kid at school by playing Keep-Away with the ball and never letting the new kid get a turn."

Decide how David can stand firm in this situation. Then choose two people to act out the situation and David's response for the rest of the class.

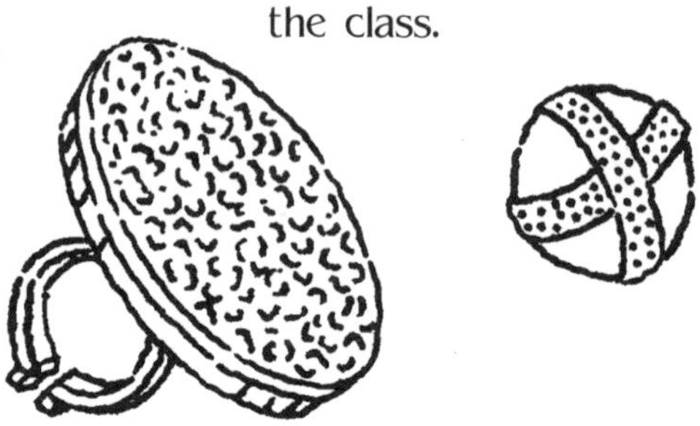

Miniature-Trophy Cheat

Beth and Bill are going to compete in a race in gym class. They're the fastest runners in class. Beth points to the trophy the teacher will award the first-place runner and says to Bill, "I really want this trophy. If you let me win, I'll give you my allowance next week."

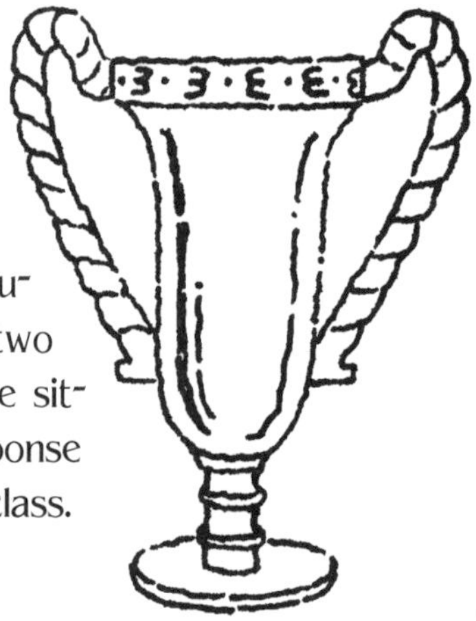

Decide how Bill can stand firm in this situation. Then choose two people to act out the situation and Bill's response for the rest of the class.

Tool-Kit Destruction

Martin and Michael borrowed a neighbor's *tool kit* and lost one of the tools. Martin holds up the *tool kit* and says, "Take this back to Mr. Frank. Don't say anything about the pliers we lost, OK?"

Decide how Michael can stand firm in this situation. Then choose two people to act out the situation and Michael's response for the rest of the class.

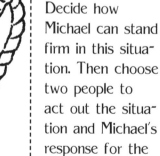

LESSON 11

TRUST GOD!

THE POINT

True heroes trust in God.

THE BIBLE BASIS

Joshua 1:1-9. God speaks to Joshua.

When God appointed Joshua to lead the Israelites into the Promised Land, he told him not once or twice but three times, "Be strong and brave." This advice must have raised all kinds of questions in Joshua's mind: What battles would he have to fight? What kind of people would he encounter? Would he be a good leader for God's people? But God also reassured Joshua: "The Lord your God will be with you everywhere you go." In spite of any doubts he might have had, Joshua knew he could trust God to help him lead the people safely.

Like Joshua, third- and fourth-graders wonder what new challenges they'll face each day. Will they get knocked down on the playground? Will people make fun of them at school? Will their grades measure up? Kids need to know that they can trust God to help them with all their struggles—even the ones that seem silly or embarrassing. Use this lesson to teach kids that if they put their trust in God, God will be with them wherever they go.

Other Scriptures used in this lesson are **Genesis 6:5-14; 22:1-13; Exodus 15:1-21; Esther 8:1-8; Psalms 23:1-6; 37:3-6; Daniel 3:10-27;** and **Luke 1:5-17, 26-38.**

GETTING THE POINT

Students will

- experience what it means to trust,
- learn how Bible characters trusted God,
- discover why God is trustworthy, and
- examine areas of their lives where they need to trust God.

THIS LESSON AT A GLANCE

Before the lesson, collect the necessary items from the Learning Lab for the activities you plan to use. Refer to the pictures in the margin to see what each item looks like.

SECTION	MINUTES	WHAT STUDENTS WILL DO	LEARNING LAB SUPPLIES	CLASSROOM SUPPLIES
ATTENTION GRABBER	up to 15	**HIGH STEPPIN'**—Run an obstacle course with a partner.	Neon kite string, terry ropes	
BIBLE EXPLORATION AND APPLICATION	up to 15	**STRONG AND BRAVE**—Read Joshua 1:1-9, then read various Scriptures and make comic books about Bible superheroes.		Bibles, newsprint, markers
	up to 10	**TOE-TO-TOE TRUST**—Pass a tool with their toes, eat a snack, and discuss Psalm 23:1-6.	Tool kit	Bible, snacks
	up to 15	**EVERY DAY, EVERY WAY**—Brainstorm ways to trust God at home, at school, and with friends, then read Psalm 37:3-6.		Bibles, newsprint, markers, tape
CLOSING	up to 5	**PROMISE RINGS**—Receive a colored ring as a sign of their promise to trust God.	Colored rings	

Hands-On FUN AT HOME

Remember to make photocopies of the "Hands-On Fun at Home" handout (p. 145) to send home with your kids. The "Fun at Home" handout suggests ways for kids to talk with their families about what they're learning in class and helps them put their faith into action.

THE LESSON

LEARNING LAB

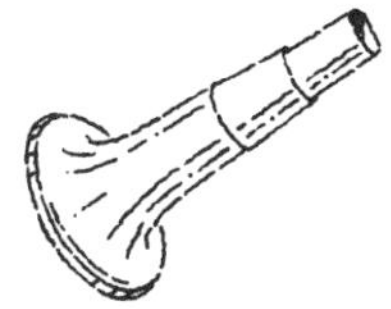

As kids arrive, ask them which "Fun at Home" activities they tried. Ask questions such as "Who did you give your 'stand-firm' footprint to? How did that person respond?" and "How did God help you stand up for what you believe?"

Tell kids that whenever you blow the *trumpet* twice, they are to stop talking, raise their hands, and focus on you. Explain that it's important to respond to this signal quickly so the class can do as many fun activities as possible.

ATTENTION GRABBER

HIGH STEPPIN'
(up to 15 minutes)

LEARNING LAB

Form two groups. Give one group the *neon kite string* and the other group the *terry ropes*. Have groups stand on opposite sides of the room.

Say to the group with the *terry ropes:* **Form pairs, then blindfold one partner in each pair with a *terry rope*. In a minute, sighted partners will give directions to safely guide their blindfolded partners through an obstacle course. Blindfold your partners while I give instructions to the other group.** If you have more than 12 students per group, have pairs share the *terry ropes*.

Say to the group with the *neon kite string:* **Form two lines facing each other, about four feet apart. Weave the string across the two lines, and behind and around your ankles to create an obstacle course for the other group. Don't wrap the string too tightly. In a minute, sighted partners from the other group will lead their blindfolded partners through the course. As they do, shout instructions to lead the blindfolded partners off course—for example, "Over this way" or "Only one foot farther."**

TEACHER TIP

If you've used most of the *neon kite string* already, use regular string or yarn for this activity.

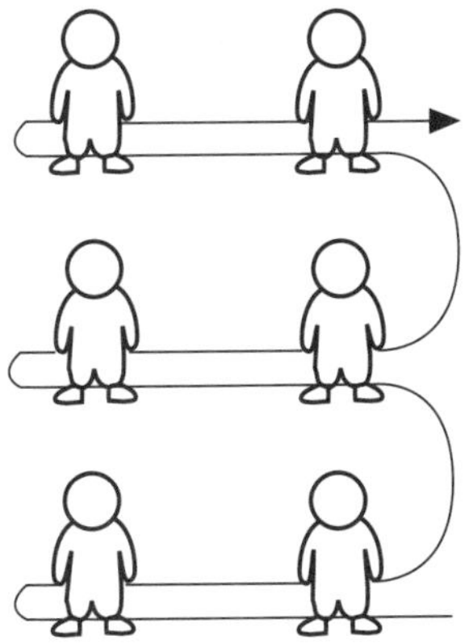

Use the margin diagram to help the group with the kite string create the obstacle course. Then say: **You'll take turns going through the obstacle course one pair at a time. Sighted partner, hold your blindfolded partner's elbow, and guide him or her through the obstacle course. Make sure neither of you steps on the string.**

Have pairs take turns stepping through the obstacle course. Encourage the obstacle-course group to give instructions that will lead the blindfolded people off course. If time permits, repeat the activity, and have groups switch roles. If you have fewer than 12 students in your class, create the obstacle course by weaving the kite string around the furniture in your room.

Blow the *trumpet* twice, and wait for kids to respond. Undo the obstacle course, and place the *neon kite string* and the *terry ropes* out of sight.

Ask:

● **What was it like to be blindfolded?** (I felt helpless; scared; nervous.)

● **What was it like to guide a blindfolded person?** (I felt responsible; I didn't want her to trip; I wanted to give good directions because he trusted me.)

● **How did you know whether to trust your partner or the people calling out directions?** (My partner was there to help me; the other group gave bad advice; my partner was really nice.)

● **How do you know who to trust in real life? Explain.** (I trust my family because they love me; I trust God; I trust people who know me.)

● **Why does God want us to trust him?** (God loves us; God knows what's best for us; God won't give us bad directions.)

the POINT

Say: **Even when we can't trust other people, we can always trust God. God will never give us bad advice or steer us the wrong way. True heroes trust in God. Today we'll learn how our hero Joshua trusted God and discover why we can trust God too.**

BIBLE EXPLORATION AND APPLICATION

STRONG AND BRAVE
(up to 15 minutes)

Write the following list of Bible references and heroes on a chalkboard or newsprint:

● **Genesis 6:5-14** (Noah)
● **Genesis 22:1-13** (Abraham)
● **Exodus 15:1-21** (Moses)
● **Esther 8:1-8** (Esther)
● **Daniel 3:10-27** (Shadrach, Meshach, and Abednego)
● **Luke 1:5-17** (Elizabeth)
● **Luke 1:26-38** (Mary)

Say: **Today we're going to look more closely at what made Joshua a hero. Let's begin right now.** Form pairs. Help kids find **Joshua 1:1-9** in their Bibles. Have kids read the passage with their partners. Encourage them to take turns reading the verses.

TEACHER TIP

Encourage active participation by following up kids' answers with questions such as "What do you mean by that?" and "Can you tell me more?"

Blow the *trumpet* twice, and wait for kids to respond. Have pairs discuss the following questions. Pause after you ask each question to allow time for discussion. Ask:

● **Why do you think God kept telling Joshua to be strong and brave?** (God wanted to give him courage; Joshua probably felt lonely and scared after Moses died.)

● **God told Joshua three times to be strong and brave. What would it be like if God gave you the same message again and again?** (I'd know God meant it; I'd remember it.)

● **Why do you think Joshua trusted God?** (Because God said he'd be with Joshua wherever he went; because God had helped the people before; Joshua knew God loved him.)

● **Why should we trust God?** (Because God promises to be with us always; because God loves us very much.)

Blow the *trumpet* twice, and wait for kids to respond. Invite them to share insights they gained from their discussions.

Say: **Joshua was one hero who trusted God. Today we see all kinds of heroes in movies, on television, and in the newspapers. We can even read about superheroes in comic books. In a minute, we're going to make our own comic books about heroes in the Bible who trusted God.**

Form four groups. Give each group two sheets of newsprint and several markers. Point to the list of passages about Bible heroes. Say: **Choose a Bible hero from the list. Take turns reading your passage. Fold your sheets of newsprint in half, and tuck one inside the other to make a book. Then design a comic book to tell about your Bible superhero. You could draw colorful action pictures, such as Shadrach, Meshach, and Abednego praying in a fiery furnace. Or you could write words that describe your heroes, such as "brave," "honest," "daring," or "faithful."**

TEACHER TIP

Encourage groups to draw comic illustrations or simple stick figures. Have them add dialogue in speech balloons and write "sound effect" words such as "zap," "boom," and "pow."

After 10 minutes, blow the *trumpet* twice, and wait for kids to respond. Have volunteers read their groups' Bible-superhero comic books to the class.

the POINT

When all groups have finished, say: **True heroes trust in God. As you can see, the Bible is full of people who trusted in God even when the situations seemed impossible! God turned average people into super, extraordinary heroes. Trust God, and you can be a hero, too!**

TOE-TO-TOE TRUST
(up to 10 minutes)

Place snacks on one side of the room. Have kids form a line on the opposite side of the room. Have kids take off their right shoes and socks. Place a tool from the *tool kit* on the floor in front of the last person in line. Say: **Pick up this tool between your big toe and the next toe, and pass it to the person on your right. Then that person will pick up the tool with his or her toes and pass it, and so on. After you've passed the tool, hop on your "shoed foot" to the front of the line, sit down, and be ready to receive the tool again. We'll keep passing and hopping until the first person in line reaches the snacks. I'll stand by to help you in any way I can.**

LEARNING LAB

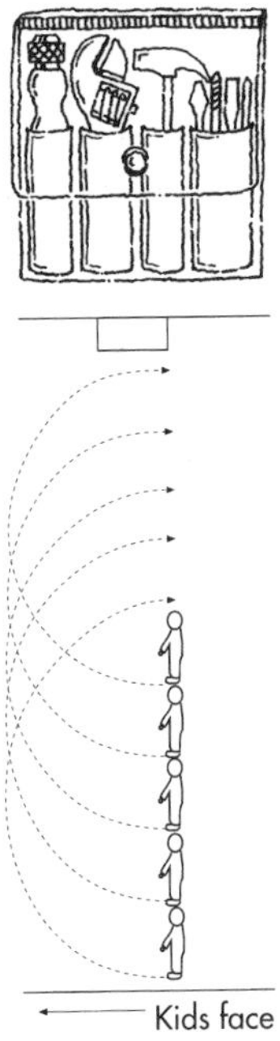

Start the game, and encourage kids to proceed toward the snacks. While kids are passing the tool, help out as much as you can. Say kind and encouraging words such as "You're doing great" or "You'll love the reward that's waiting for you." If a person drops the tool, pick it up, and

TEACHER TIP

If you have girls in your class who are wearing tights, or if kids don't want to remove their socks, have them hold and pass the tool between their feet.

TEACHER TIP

It's important to say The Point just as it's written in each activity. Repeating The Point over and over will help kids remember it and apply it to their lives.

the POINT

replace it between his or her toes.

When the first person in line reaches the snacks, have kids put their shoes and socks back on. Say encouraging words as you serve the snacks, such as "Good job," "I knew you could do it," and "I like the way you cooperate." While kids are eating, ask:

- **How did I help you during the game?** (You said nice things; you picked up the tool when it dropped; you gave us good snacks.)
- **How was the way I helped you during the game like the way God helps you in real life?** (God helps me when I mess up; God encourages me and makes me feel good.)

Say: **Let's read a passage in the Bible that talks about some of the ways God helps us. I'll read the passage since you're still eating your snacks.**

Read aloud **Psalm 23:1-6.** Ask:

- **According to this passage, what are some ways that God helps us?** (God helps us do right; God gives us what we need; he's with us all the time.)
- **How was God like a shepherd to Joshua?** (God led him into the Promised Land; God took care of him.)
- **How is God like a shepherd to us?** (God loves us and cares for us as a shepherd cares for his sheep; God watches over us and keeps us safe.)
- **Why should we trust God to help us?** (Because God knows what's best for us; because other people might lead us the wrong way.)

Say: **We can trust God to help us in any situation. Even when we don't think about him, God is with us, leading us in the right direction. True heroes trust in God. That's because they know God is their shepherd and will always lead them the right way. Let's discover some specific times and places we can trust God.**

Place the *tool kit* out of sight for use in future lessons.

EVERY DAY, EVERY WAY
(up to 15 minutes)

Form three groups. Have each group sit in a circle. Say: **In Psalm 37, David talks about trusting God. Let's turn to that passage now.** Help kids find **Psalm 37:3-6** in their Bibles. Have a volunteer read aloud the passage. Encourage others to follow along in their Bibles.

Have each group choose a recorder, a reporter, and an encourager. If you have more than three students in each group, assign more encouragers. Give each recorder a sheet of newsprint and a marker. Assign each group either "home," "school," or "friends." Have recorders write their assigned area in large letters at the top of their newsprint.

Say: **Our good shepherd, God, wants us to trust him every day and in every way—at home, at school, and with our friends. Brainstorm at least five ways to trust God in your group's area. For example, at home you could trust God to keep your family safe, at**

school you could trust God to help you do your best on a test, and with friends you could trust God to help you choose the best friends and be the best friend possible. Recorders, write down your group's ideas on the sheet of newsprint. Encouragers, urge your group members to contribute ideas to the conversation. Reporters, you will read your group's ideas to the rest of the class.

After about three minutes, blow the *trumpet* twice, and wait for kids to respond. Have reporters tape their sheets of newsprint to the wall and read their groups' ideas to the class. Ask:

- **Why is it difficult to trust God in these areas?** (Because I can't see God; I want to do things my own way; because my friends don't understand about trusting God.)
- **Think about our hero, Joshua. Do you think he ever had trouble trusting God? Explain?** (Yes, he might have had trouble trusting God to help him defeat other armies; no, Joshua always trusted God.)
- **What happens when we decide to trust God?** (We feel better; we know we're doing the right thing; God helps us take care of our problems.)
- **In which area is it hardest for you to trust God? Explain.** (School, because it gets so hard sometimes; home, because my parents argue; with my friends, because I want them to know Jesus, too.)

Say: **Look at the lists, and choose one area where you need to learn to trust God. For example, you could trust God to help a parent get a job. Pray about that area with the people in your groups. Start by saying, "Dear God, we trust you to help us in these areas..." Then go around your group and have each person pray for the area he or she chose. You can close by saying "amen" together.**

Pause while groups pray. After all the groups have said "amen," blow the *trumpet* twice, and wait for kids to respond. Say: **We can trust God, our Shepherd, to guide us and help us. True heroes trust in God. God helps you at home, at school, and with your friends—every day and every way.**

the POINT

Hands-On Fun at Home

We believe that Christian education extends beyond the classroom into the home. Photocopy the "Hands-On Fun at Home" handout (p. 145) for this week, and send it home with your kids. Encourage kids to try several activities and discuss the Bible verses and questions with their parents.

CLOSING

LEARNING LAB

> **TEACHER TIP**
>
> If you have more students than *colored rings,* form additional rings out of rolled aluminum foil or string.

the POINT

PROMISE RINGS
(up to 5 minutes)

Say: **We've learned about Bible heroes who trusted God. We've talked about trusting God at home, at school, and with our friends—every day and every way. Now let's close by making trusting promises.**

Have kids stand in a large circle. Bring out the *colored rings* and say: **Rings are used to symbolize a promise. For example, in weddings a man and woman exchange rings and promise to love each other. Let's use these rings to make trusting promises to ourselves and to God. Complete this sentence: "I'll be a hero for God. I promise to trust God the next time I . . ." For example, you might fill in the blank with "take a test," "hear my parents fight," or "go on a trip." If someone gets stuck, we'll all offer ideas. When you say your promise, I'll place a *colored ring* on your finger to remind you to trust God.**

Go around the circle and let everyone complete the sentence and receive a ring. Then say: **True heroes trust in God. I know you'll all be true heroes and remember your promise to trust in God this week.**

Encourage kids to take home their rings as reminders of their promises.

Hands-On FUN AT HOME

LESSON 11: TRUST GOD!

the POINT True heroes trust in God.

BIBLE FOCUS

"Be strong and brave. Don't be afraid, because the Lord your God will be with you everywhere you go" (Joshua 1:9).

NOTABLES

Write on this note one worry that you'll trust God to help you with this week. Cut out the note, and put it on your bulletin board, refrigerator, or mirror—any place where you'll see it every day. Whenever you start to worry, look at the note, and remember that God has you in the palms of his hands. You can trust him!

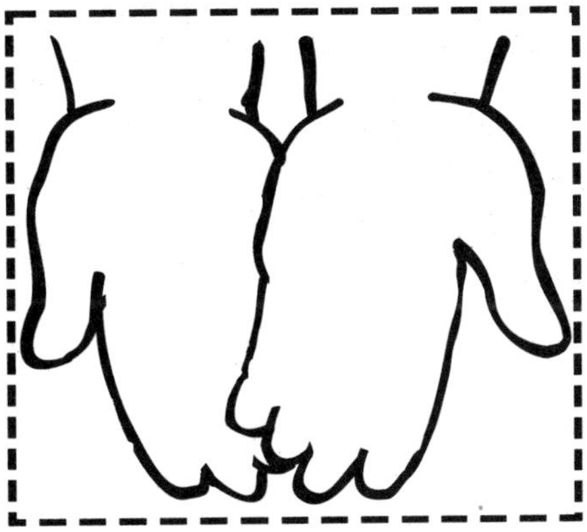

CHECK it OUT

Read Psalm 20:7.
What other things do people trust in instead of God? Why is it important to trust in only God?

Read Isaiah 25:9.
How does trusting in God make you happy?

Read John 12:35-36.
How is trusting God like walking in the light?

LAUGH it UP

OF COURSE I TRUST YOU!
YA-HOO!

FAITH walk

Missionaries are true heroes. They have to trust God for food, clothes, money, housing, and safety as they share God's Word with people around the world. Your family can help a missionary family by praying, writing letters, and sending money each month. Contact your church for information about a missionary family your family can help support. Trusting God together, you can really make a difference!

LESSON 12

GOING GOD'S WAY

THE POINT

True heroes follow God's directions.

THE BIBLE BASIS

Joshua 3:1–4:24. Joshua leads the people across the Jordan River.

God told Joshua, "Today I will begin to make you great in the opinion of all the Israelites so the people will know I am with you just as I was with Moses" (Joshua 3:7). God commanded Joshua to lead the Israelites across the Jordan River. Joshua was a true hero who followed God's directions. God caused the water to stop flowing so the Israelites could cross the river. That day, God made Joshua great in the eyes of the Israelites. They respected Joshua all his life, just as they had respected Moses.

It's hard enough for adults, let alone third- and fourth-graders, to follow God's directions. God says, "Obey your parents," but parents aren't always perfect. God says, "Love one another," but some people just aren't very lovable. God says, "Be kind and compassionate," but sometimes it's tempting to tease. Many of today's media heroes ignore God, so kids may think they can ignore God too. Use this lesson to help kids learn the value of following God's directions.

Other Scriptures used in this lesson are **Psalm 119:1-5** and **Proverbs 3:5-6.**

GETTING THE POINT

Students will

- explore what the Bible says about following God's directions,
- follow directions that lead to an affirmation treasure, and
- discover that God's directions always lead to good things.

THIS LESSON AT A GLANCE

Before the lesson, collect the necessary items from the Learning Lab for the activities you plan to use. Refer to the pictures in the margin to see what each item looks like.

SECTION	MINUTES	WHAT STUDENTS WILL DO	LEARNING LAB SUPPLIES	CLASSROOM SUPPLIES
ATTENTION GRABBER	up to 10	**FOLLOWING DIRECTIONS—**Run a relay by following directions.	Miniature trophy, plastic eggs, prism shapes	
BIBLE EXPLORATION AND APPLICATION	up to 10	**DAFFY DIRECTIONS—**Follow silly directions, receive rewards, and read Proverbs 3:5-6.		Bibles, "Daffy Directions" handout (p. 155), snacks
	up to 15	**REMEMBER THE RIVER—**Act out the Bible story in Joshua 3:1–4:24.	Cassette: "Remember the River"	Bible, "Remember the River" handout (p. 156), cassette player
	up to 15	**AFFIRMATION TREASURE HUNT—**Hide treasures, make maps, and read Psalm 119:1-5.	Learning Lab box and all items	Bibles, pencils, paper, tape
CLOSING	up to 10	**ROCKS OF REMEMBRANCE—**Make symbols to remind themselves of God's love and care.	Celluclay	Wax paper or aluminum foil, scissors

Hands-On FUN AT HOME

Remember to make photocopies of the "Hands-On Fun at Home" handout (p. 157) to send home with your kids. The "Fun at Home" handout suggests ways for kids to talk with their families about what they're learning in class and helps them put their faith into action.

THE LESSON

LEARNING LAB

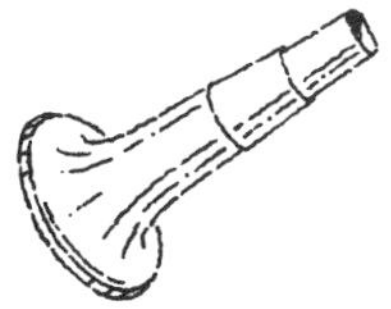

As kids arrive, ask them which "Fun at Home" activities they tried. Ask questions such as "What plans did you make to help a missionary family?" and "What worry did you trust God to help you with?"

Tell kids that whenever you blow the *trumpet* twice, they are to stop talking, raise their hands, and focus on you. Explain that it's important to respond to this signal quickly so the class can do as many fun activities as possible.

ATTENTION GRABBER

FOLLOWING DIRECTIONS
(up to 10 minutes)

LEARNING LAB

Take two volunteers aside, and say: **I'm going to give the class directions to run a relay. Your job is to offer kids directions that are different from my directions. I'll tell the kids to roll a *plastic egg* with their noses, take one *prism shape* from the egg, place the shape in the *miniature trophy,* then roll the egg back to their teams. As a person reaches the trophy during the race, you'll say, "Pick up the egg and run back!" or "Put two *prism shapes* in the trophy—not just one!"**

Place the *miniature trophy* on the floor at one end of the classroom. Form two teams, and have each team form a line at the opposite end of the room. Have the volunteers stand by the trophy. Give the first person in each line a *plastic egg* filled with 10 *prism shapes.*

Say: **To start the relay, I'll say, "Roll those eggs." If you're the first person on your team, get on your hands and knees, and use your nose to roll your *plastic egg* across the room to the trophy. Open your egg, take out one *prism shape,* put it in the *miniature trophy,* close the egg, and use your nose to roll it back to the next team member. Then the next person in line will do the same thing until everyone has had a turn. The first team to follow my directions and complete the race wins. The two volunteers standing across the room will watch to be sure you put the shape in the trophy. Ready? Put your nose to the ground and roll those eggs!**

If a person follows the directions of a volunteer rather than your directions, that person is disqualified from play. After all the team members have completed the relay, blow the *trumpet* twice, and wait for kids to respond. Declare a winner. Collect the *miniature trophy, plastic eggs,* and *prism shapes* for use in future lessons. Have kids sit in a circle, then ask:

- **What did you think about the volunteers' directions?** (I was confused; I knew they were lying.)

TEACHER TIP

If your classroom is small, you may want to do this activity in a fellowship hall or large meeting room.

TEACHER TIP

If you have fewer than eight students in your class, choose one volunteer to stand by the *miniature trophy,* and have the rest of the students form one line to run the relay.

● **How did you decide whose directions to follow?** (I didn't think you'd notice if I followed their instructions; you said we had to follow your directions to win.)

● **How is following directions in this game like following God's directions?** (Different people tell you to do different things; God's directions are sometimes hard to follow; people try to get you to turn away from God's directions.)

the POINT ☞

Say: ☞ **True heroes follow God's directions. Sometimes people try to get us to do the opposite of what God wants us to do, just as the two volunteers in our game did. But when we listen to God, he always leads us to good things because he loves us and wants what's best for us. Today we're going to discover why God's directions are so good.**

BIBLE EXPLORATION AND APPLICATION

DAFFY DIRECTIONS
(up to 10 minutes)

Before class, photocopy the "Daffy Directions" handout (p. 155), then cut apart the directions. You'll need one direction for each student. Place a container of snacks, such as doughnut holes or fruit, out of sight.

Distribute the directions. Have kids form a line along one end of the room. Stand at the opposite end of the room, then say: **One at a time, read aloud your direction, do what it says, then take the number of steps it says to take toward me. Follow your direction even if it seems silly. When everyone has had a turn, I'll ask you to exchange directions with the person standing closest to you. Then we'll continue by reading and following the new directions until someone reaches me. Although it may seem silly, this game will produce a good result. Trust me!**

When someone reaches you, say: **All right! Because you followed your directions so well, everyone will receive a snack as a reward!**

Have kids sit in pairs. Distribute the snacks. Have pairs discuss the following questions while they eat. Ask:

● **What was it like to follow the directions?** (Fun; I didn't understand why I had to do it; I liked seeing other kids follow their directions.)

● **How did you feel when you learned you'd get a snack for a reward?** (Great; hungry; glad I followed my direction.)

● **How was following these directions like following God's directions?** (We get a reward when we follow God; we had to trust you like we have to trust God; God's directions aren't this weird.)

When kids have finished eating their snacks, say: **Following God's directions is always better than relying on our own ideas. Let's look in the book of Proverbs to find out why.** Help kids find

Proverbs 3:5-6. Have pairs take turns reading the verses. Pause after you ask each of the following questions and allow time for discussion. Ask:

- **What does Proverbs 3:5-6 tell us about following God's directions?** (Trust God to lead us; God will give us success; remember God and trust him with all our heart.)
- **What's wrong with depending on our own understanding?** (We don't know everything; God is leading us, and he knows the way; we don't always understand what God wants us to do.)
- **What does it mean to trust God with all our heart?** (Listen to him; follow God's directions; believe that he will take care of us.)
- **Why is it sometimes hard to trust God to lead us?** (Because we don't understand what God wants us to do; because we want to do things our way; God's way might be harder.)
- **How can we trust God and follow his directions?** (Read the Bible; pray; ask advice from parents and teachers.)

Blow the *trumpet* twice to bring everyone together. Wait for kids to respond, then invite them to share insights from their discussions.

Say: **True heroes follow God's directions. Sometimes even heroes don't understand what God's directions mean or where they're leading. But depending on our own understanding doesn't get us very far. That's why it's important to pray, read the Bible, ask advice from other Christians, and trust that God will help us understand. Let's hear a story about someone who followed God's directions and became a hero!**

TEACHER TIP

It's important to say The Point just as it's written in each activity. Repeating The Point over and over will help kids remember it and apply it to their lives.

the POINT

REMEMBER THE RIVER
(up to 15 minutes)

LEARNING LAB

Make one photocopy of the "Remember the River" handout (p. 156). Then cue the *cassette tape* to the "Remember the River" segment.

Say: **Our Bible story comes from Joshua 3:1–4:24.** Open your Bible and show kids the passage. Give a volunteer the photocopy of the "Remember the River" handout. As you play the "Remember the River" segment of the *cassette tape,* have the volunteer pantomime the story. Say: **God's directions may not have made much sense at first to this Bible hero. Listen carefully and watch** (name) **pantomime the story. Then I'll play the story again, and we'll all act it out.**

Play "Remember the River" from the *cassette tape*. After the story, rewind the tape to the beginning of the segment. Then say: **Now that we're familiar with this story, let's act it out together as we listen to the tape again. I need another volunteer to lead us.**

After kids have acted out the story, have them sit in a circle. Ask:

- **Which of God's directions might have been hard to understand?** (That the priests had to lead them across the water; that they had to pick out 12 rocks.)
- **Why do you think Joshua followed God's directions?** (Because he loved and trusted God; because he'd seen God's miracles; because he didn't know what else to do.)

● **What might have happened if Joshua hadn't followed God's directions?** (God would've been angry; the people would've been stuck at the river; the people wouldn't have thought so much of Joshua.)

● **What happens when we don't follow God's directions?** (We do the wrong thing; we get frustrated; it makes God sad.)

● **How do you feel when you do follow God's directions?** (Good; happy; like I know I'm doing the right thing.)

the POINT

Say: **True heroes follow God's directions. Because God loves us, he always leads us in the right direction.**

LEARNING LAB

AFFIRMATION TREASURE HUNT
(up to 15 minutes)

Form four groups. Set out pencils, paper, tape, and the Learning Lab box with all the items in it. Say: **To learn how important directions are, we're going to go on a treasure hunt! Each group will hide a treasure and create a treasure map. As a group, select an item from the Learning Lab box to be your treasure. Think of a fun way to use that item to affirm the group you'll trade maps with. For example, you might take the *tool kit* and attach a note that says, "You guys 'fix' up a dull class." Or you might attach a note to the *miniature trophy* that says, "The great hero award. You guys follow God's directions." After you attach an affirmation to your treasure, hide it on a shelf or in a closet, drawer, or hallway. Then draw a map on your sheet of paper to lead others to your treasure!**

TEACHER TIP

If groups have trouble thinking of affirmations, suggest these ideas:

- A note attached to a *prism shape* that reads, "You are all sparkling stars."
- A note attached to a *terry rope* that reads, "Have your group members wrap this rope around themselves and imagine it's a hug. You are wonderful."
- A note attached to the *spy disguise* that reads, "There's no disguising it. God really loves you."

After each group chooses an item from the Learning Lab box, allow about five minutes for groups to attach affirmations to their treasures, hide them, then draw their maps. After five minutes, blow the *trumpet* twice, and wait for kids to respond.

Say: **Trade maps with another group. Then follow the map, and find the treasure. When you find it, bring it back and sit in a circle.**

When all groups have found their treasures and are sitting in the circle, have volunteers share their groups' affirmation treasures. Ask:

● **What was it like to follow the directions on the treasure map?** (Fun; it was easy to read and follow; it led right to the treasure; we had a hard time figuring out the map.)

● **How did you feel when you found the treasure?** (Happy; relieved; proud.)

Say: **We have a map that can lead to treasure in our lives. It's called the Bible.** Help kids find **Psalm 119:1-5** in their Bibles. Have a volunteer read the passage aloud. Encourage others to follow along in their Bibles. Ask:

● **How is following God's Word like following a treasure map?** (They both lead to something good; God's Word is like a map that tells us which way to go; sometimes they both can be confusing.)

● **Why is the Bible sometimes hard to follow?** (Because we don't understand it; we get confused.)

● **How can we learn to understand and follow the Bible?** (Study it at Sunday school; read it with our parents and ask questions when we don't understand; learn things in church that will help us understand.)

● **What are some of the treasures we find when we read the Bible and follow God's directions?** (God's promises; knowing that Jesus died for us; learning that God loves us.)

the POINT

Say: **True heroes follow God's directions. Those directions are given to us right here in the Bible—God's Word. Reading the Bible is like following a map made by God that leads us to wonderful treasures!**

Hands-On FUN AT HOME

We believe that Christian education extends beyond the classroom into the home. Photocopy the "Hands-On Fun at Home" handout (p. 157) for this week, and send it home with your kids. Encourage kids to try several activities and discuss the Bible verses and questions with their parents.

CLOSING

ROCKS OF REMEMBRANCE
(up to 10 minutes)

LEARNING LAB

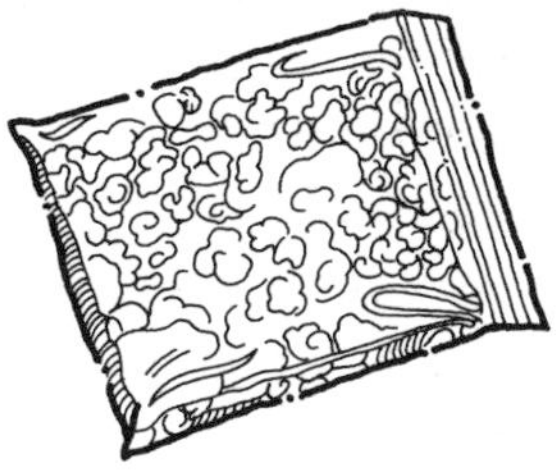

Ask:

● **What did you learn today?** (We learned about Joshua, who followed God's directions; we discovered that God's Word leads to a treasure; we found out how important it is to follow God's directions.)

Say: **Now let's close by thinking about how God has worked in our lives.**

Form pairs. Say: **Tell your partner how God encouraged you and took care of you during a hard time. For example, maybe you were lonely because your best friend moved away, then God sent a new friend into your life.**

After two minutes, blow the *trumpet* twice, and wait for kids to respond. Say: **When we remember how God encouraged us and took care of us in the past, it's easier to trust and follow God's directions in the future. Remember how God told Joshua to have 12 men choose 12 rocks as a reminder that God helped them cross the Jordan River? We'll use this *Celluclay* to help us remember how God cares for us.**

Give each person a 6-inch square of wax paper or aluminum foil. Say: **We'll each form a shape to symbolize God's love and care. For**

example, you might make a circle shape to show that God's care never ends, a heart shape to show God's love, or a cross shape to show Jesus' forgiveness. Poke a hole in your shape. Next week, we'll decorate the shapes, then thread yarn or string through them to make medallions.

Open the bag of *Celluclay,* and add one-half cup of warm water. Close the bag and knead until mixture reaches the consistency of clay or stiff dough. Then let kids take turns squeezing shapes onto their foil or wax paper squares. Encourage kids to keep their shapes small so you'll have enough *Celluclay* for everyone. Have kids set their shapes on a table to dry, then have the kids form a circle around the table. Say: **One at a time, point out your shape, and tell us what it symbolizes.**

TEACHER TIP

If you have enough *Celluclay,* make a few extra shapes for visitors and kids who are absent.

After each person shares, leave the shapes to dry overnight. If you can, leave the shapes in your classroom until next week. If someone else will be using your room, ask a church worker to carefully remove and store the shapes until your next meeting.

the POINT

Say: **Good job! Now, let's close in prayer. Dear God, we know that true heroes follow your directions. Help us to remember the great things you did for us in the past and to trust you to do great things in the future. Help us to follow your directions. We know you'll always give us the right directions because you love us. In Jesus' name, amen.**

Daffy Directions

Say your favorite hobby and why you enjoy it, then take two giant steps toward the teacher.

Spin around four times, then take three giant steps toward the teacher.

Do three jumping jacks, then take two tiny steps toward the teacher.

Link arms with someone and take four giant steps toward the teacher.

Sing "Happy Birthday to You" to yourself, then take one giant step toward the teacher.

Tell about your best family vacation, then take four tiny steps toward the teacher.

As loudly as you can, clap five times, then take one giant step toward the teacher.

Tell a joke, then take three tiny steps toward the teacher.

Crow like a rooster, then take five steps toward the teacher.

Describe your favorite Bible character, then take two giant steps toward the teacher.

Remember the River

Listen to this story on the *cassette tape.* As you hear the words in the left column, lead the class in doing the actions in the right column.

The Lord said to Joshua, "Today I will begin to make you great in the opinion of all the Israelites so the people will know I am with you just as I was with Moses."	***Point to your chest, look surprised, and silently say, "Me?"***
The Lord said to Joshua, "Tell the priests who carry the Ark of the Covenant to go to the edge of the Jordan River and stand in the water."	***Hold a hand to your ear, and silently say, "What?"***
Joshua thought, "OK, God. I may not understand, but I'll follow your directions."	***Shrug your shoulders, then give a thumbs-up sign.***
Joshua told the Israelites, "The priests will carry the Ark into the Jordan River ahead of you."	***Bend down, and pretend to pick up a heavy object.***
"When the priests step into the water, it will stop flowing."	***Scratch your head, and look puzzled.***
So the people left the place where they had camped, and they followed the priests who carried the Ark. When the priests came to the edge of the river and stepped into the water, the water upstream stopped flowing.	***Put your hands out in front of you as if you're stopping the water.***
The priests stood in the middle of the river on dry ground and waited there while all the people of Israel walked across on dry land.	***Motion with your arm for people to follow you.***
After the people had crossed, the Lord said to Joshua, "Choose 12 men to get 12 rocks from the middle of the river."	***Count to 12 on your fingers.***
So Joshua chose one man from each of the 12 tribes to go to the river and bring back 12 rocks. The Israelites obeyed Joshua and carried the 12 rocks with them and put them down where they made their camp.	***Pretend to carry a huge rock, then set it down.***
Joshua told the Israelites, "In the future, your children will ask you, 'What do these rocks mean?' "	***Point, then scratch your head.***
"Tell them, 'Israel crossed the Jordan River on dry land. God caused the water to stop flowing until the people crossed.' "	***Point to heaven with one hand, then push the other hand out to signal "stop."***
That day the Lord made Joshua great in the opinion of all the Israelites. They respected Joshua all his life, just as they had respected Moses.	***Gently pat a neighbor's back.***

LESSON 12:
GOING GOD'S WAY

the POINT True heroes follow God's directions.

Hands-On FUN AT HOME

BIBLE FOCUS

"Be strong and brave. Don't be afraid, because the Lord your God will be everywhere you go" (Joshua 1:9).

WAY to PRAY

Read about four disciples who followed Jesus' directions in Mark 1:16-20. Then join hands with your family members. Take turns saying one way you want to follow God's directions this week; for example, you might say "I want to read the Bible more," "I want to ask my new neighbor to come to church with me," or "I want to make a cake and give it to Grandma." After each person has had a turn, have each person pray, "God, help me follow you this week." End by saying "amen" together and having a giant family hug.

LAUGH it UP

THIS WILL BE EASY!
DIRECTIONS
MODEL PLANE

FAITH walk

Give each family member a sheet of paper. Have each person create a treasure map to follow this week, drawing dotted lines that lead to directions such as "Monday: Hug a family member," "Tuesday: Do my best work at school," and "Wednesday: Read a chapter in the Bible." Make the treasure at the end of each map be your family's favorite meal. Then, switch maps with each other, and follow the directions. At the end of the week, cook and eat the "treasure meal" together, and talk about what happens when you follow good directions.

CHECK it OUT

Read John 10:3-5.
This verse talks about how sheep know the shepherd's voice and follow it. How do you follow Jesus?

Read Jonah 1:1-17.
Describe a time it was hard for you to follow God's directions. What happened?

Read Galatians 6:9.
What are some good things that come from following God's directions?

LESSON 13

SHOW THEM THE WAY

THE POINT

True heroes encourage others to follow God.

THE BIBLE BASIS

Joshua 2:1-21; 6:1-27. Joshua spares Rahab because she helped and encouraged the spies.

Before the battle of Jericho, Joshua sent two spies to look at the land. Rahab hid the two spies on her roof. To an outsider, Rahab may have seemed dishonest and traitorous because she turned her back on her people and helped the Israelites destroy her city. But Rahab and the people of Jericho had heard stories of the Red Sea miraculously drying up and of kingdoms being destroyed at the Israelites' hands. These stories turned Rahab's heart toward God. She risked all she had to follow the Israelites' awesome God. Because she helped and encouraged the spies, Joshua spared Rahab and her family during the defeat of Jericho.

Like Rahab, third- and fourth-graders must decide who to follow. Heroes today encourage kids to do a variety of things—buy athletic shoes, drink soft drinks, watch certain movies, or wear a particular brand of clothes. Some heroes use their status to encourage kids to stay in school, avoid drugs, and read more books. But how many heroes encourage others to follow Jesus? Use this lesson to help kids discover that a true hero is someone who leads others toward God.

Other Scriptures used in this lesson are **Joshua 2:1-21; 6:1-27; Matthew 5:14-16; 1 Thessalonians 2:11-12; Titus 2:7-8;** and **James 3:17-18.**

GETTING THE POINT

Students will

- find out how it feels to encourage others and to be encouraged,
- explore what the Bible says about encouraging others to follow God, and
- reward one another for true heroism.

THIS LESSON AT A GLANCE

Before the lesson, collect the necessary items from the Learning Lab for the activities you plan to use. Refer to the pictures in the margin to see what each item looks like.

SECTION	MINUTES	WHAT STUDENTS WILL DO	LEARNING LAB SUPPLIES	CLASSROOM SUPPLIES
ATTENTION GRABBER	up to 10	**ALL-OUT ENCOURAGEMENT**—Encourage each other while they play a game.	Paper balls, terry ropes	
BIBLE EXPLORATION AND APPLICATION	up to 11	**TEAMWORK**—Perform tasks while linked in a circle and read Joshua 2:1-21 and 1 Thessalonians 2:11-12.	Terry ropes	Bibles
	up to 13	**TUMBLING DOWN**—Act out the story of the battle of Jericho from Joshua 6:1-27.	Trumpets	Bibles
	up to 13	**SUPERHEROES**—Brainstorm ways to encourage others to follow God and read Matthew 5:14-16; Titus 2:7-8; and James 3:17-18.		Bibles, "Hold Up the Light" handouts (p. 168), pencils, newsprint, markers, tape
CLOSING	up to 13	**HERO AWARDS**—Decorate awards and participate in an awards ceremony.	Cassette: "Hero Award," neon kite string	Cassette player, Celluclay shapes from Lesson 12, scissors, markers, construction paper

Hands-On FUN AT HOME

Remember to make photocopies of the "Hands-On Fun at Home" handout (p. 169) to send home with your kids. The "Fun at Home" handout suggests ways for kids to talk with their families about what they're learning in class and helps them put their faith into action.

THE LESSON

LEARNING LAB

As kids arrive, ask them which "Fun at Home" activities they tried. Ask questions such as "What was it like following your unique treasure map?" and "What did the Bible passages teach you about following God's directions?"

Tell kids that whenever you blow the *trumpet* twice, they are to stop talking, raise their hands, and focus on you. Explain that it's important to respond to this signal quickly so the class can do as many fun activities as possible.

MODULE REVIEW

Use the casual interaction time at the beginning of class to ask kids the following module-review questions.

- **Did you have to stand up for what you believe this week? If so, how did you find the courage and strength to do it?**
- **What worries can you trust God with? How does trusting God help you handle your worries?**
- **Have you experienced any good results because you followed God's directions? Explain.**
- **What is the most important thing you've learned in this class during the past few weeks? Why?**
- **How is your life different because of what we've learned in class this month?**

ATTENTION GRABBER

ALL-OUT ENCOURAGEMENT
(up to 10 minutes)

LEARNING LAB

Form three teams, and give each team a *terry rope*. Evenly distribute the *paper balls* among the three teams.

Say: **Form a circle on the floor with your *terry rope.* Then have everyone in your team stand around the circle about six feet back. When I say, "You can do it!" take turns tossing your *paper balls* into the circle. Each *paper ball* may be tossed only once. If one lands outside of the circle, you must leave it there. After one minute, I'll blow the *trumpet* twice. Then you'll count the number of balls inside your circle. Balls outside the circle or touching the *terry rope* don't count. There is only one more rule: You have to encourage each other for the entire minute. Say things such as "Good job," "Good throw," and "That's OK. You can do it next time." Ready? You can do it!**

After a minute, blow the *trumpet* twice, and wait for kids to respond. Say: **Good job, all of you ball tossers! Now count the number of balls in the middle of your circle.**

> **TEACHER TIP**
>
> While kids are playing the game, join in with encouraging words such as "Nice try!" and "Wow! What a shot." Encourage students to affirm each other for the entire time.

See which team tossed the most balls into its circle. Then have all students clap for themselves and say, "Way to toss!"

Place the *paper balls* out of sight. You'll need the *terry ropes* in the next activity. Have kids sit in a large circle, then ask:

● **What was it like to encourage each other through the entire game? Explain.** (Great, I like making people feel good; I couldn't think of encouraging things to say; it was fun.)

● **How do people encourage you in real life?** (They're interested in what I do; they compliment me; they love me and care for me.)

● **What do people who love you encourage you to do?** (Study; practice my piano lessons; be friendly; write letters to my grandparents.)

Say: **Our family and friends encourage us to do many good things. It's especially good when they encourage us to follow God.** Ask:

● **How do people encourage you to follow God?** (They're interested in what I learn at church; they invite me to come with them to fun events at their churches; they pray for me; they help me remember to read my Bible.)

the POINT

Say: **We can encourage each other to follow God in the same way that you encouraged each other to play the game well. True heroes encourage others to follow God. Today we're going to learn how we can do that. Amazing things happen when we encourage each other. Right now, let's find out how encouragement changed Rahab's life and how it affected an entire city.**

BIBLE EXPLORATION AND APPLICATION

LEARNING LAB

TEAMWORK
(up to 11 minutes)

Distribute Bibles and help kids find **Joshua 2:1-21.** Ask volunteers to read three verses each. Encourage others to follow along in their Bibles. Ask:

● **How did Rahab help the spies?** (She was nice to them; she helped them climb down a wall with a rope; she worked with them.)

● **What encouraged Rahab to follow the Israelites' God?** (She had heard of the miracles; she knew God had dried up the Red Sea.)

Say: **Rahab wanted to follow God because she had heard about all the miraculous things he had done for the Israelites. Rahab helped the spies, and Joshua and the Israelites were able to defeat Jericho. Now let's practice a little helping and encouraging ourselves.**

> **TEACHER TIP**
>
> If you have fewer than 10 kids, tie fewer *terry ropes* together and make a smaller circle.

Tie the six *terry ropes* together so they form a rope circle. Gather the kids and say: **Let's link ourselves together by gently wrapping the rope around one hand so we have one complete circle of people.**

Pause while kids wrap the rope around their hands, then say: **I'm**

going to give you a task to perform. Encourage and help each other. Work as a team so everyone accomplishes the task together.

Read the following tasks, and add some of your own. Feel free to adapt them to fit your classroom.

- **Walk to the center of the room, sit down, stand up, and walk back to where you started.**
- **Walk to a table, sit under it, shout, "Good job!" then walk back to where you started.**
- **Walk around a chair five times. Say, "You can do it" each time you go around.**
- **Walk quietly out of the room to a drinking fountain, let each person get a drink, then walk back.**
- **Pat the back of the person on your right, and say, "You're a true hero."**
- **Shake the hand of the person on your left, and say, "You're an encourager."**

When the tasks have been completed, have kids sit in a circle and unwrap their hands. Place the *terry ropes* out of sight. Ask:

- **What was it like to accomplish these tasks together?** (It was fun; I liked working together; it was hard to do everything together.)
- **How did you help and encourage each other?** (We talked to each other; we went slowly; we said good things to each other.)
- **How was the way you helped each other in this activity like the way Rahab helped the spies?** (She was nice to them; she helped them; she worked with them.)

Say: **Let's read what the Bible says about how to encourage friends.**

Read **1 Thessalonians 2:11-12.** Ask:

- **How do you help and encourage others to follow God?** (I tell them about God; I show God's love by giving money and clothes to people; I read Bible stories to my little brother.)

Say: **True heroes encourage others to follow God. We can do that by telling others about God, by letting God's love shine in all we do, and by working together with other Christians as we did in our game. Rahab helped and encouraged the spies, and Joshua and his people were able to conquer the city. Joshua was also a true hero who encouraged others. Let's read more about Joshua.**

> **TEACHER TIP**
>
> It's important to say The Point just as it's written in each activity. Repeating The Point over and over will help kids remember it and apply it to their lives.

the POINT

TUMBLING DOWN
(up to 13 minutes)

LEARNING LAB

Choose a volunteer to be Joshua, and have the rest of the class form these sound effects groups.

Group 1: the people inside Jericho
Group 2: the trumpet blowers
Group 3: the walls
Group 4: the Israelites

TEACHER TIP

It's OK to have one child per group. If you have fewer than five kids, have one child take more than one part.

Have the groups each read **Joshua 6:1-27** and decide on a group sound effect. For example, the people inside Jericho could make a slamming sound and a shivering-in-fear noise, the trumpet blowers could use the *trumpets* from the Learning Lab, the walls could grunt when they're standing firm then say "crash" when they're falling down, and the Israelites could make marching sounds and cheer when the walls fall down. Have Joshua say "shh" at the appropriate places in the story and "You can shout!" the seventh time the people march around the city.

After kids read the story and decide on their sound effects, blow the *trumpet* twice, and wait for kids to respond. Then say: **Now that we're familiar with this story, let's put sounds to it.**

Position groups a few feet apart from each other. Have Joshua stand near the Israelites and the trumpet blowers.

Give the *trumpets* to the trumpet blowers. Tell the following story, and have kids perform their sound effects when you pause.

The people of Jericho were afraid of Joshua's army because they had heard what God had done for the Israelites. Pause. **The people closed the gates to their city and didn't come in or go out.** Pause.

God planned to give the city of Jericho to Joshua and the Israelites. God told the Israelite people to march around the city of Jericho once a day for six days. Pause.

The people of Jericho were still afraid, even though their city stood and the Israelites hadn't attacked. Pause.

On the seventh day, Joshua, the priests, and the Israelites began marching around the walls of Jericho seven more times.

The trumpets sounded as the people marched around the walls of Jericho the first time that day, but the city walls stood firm. Pause.

Joshua told his people, "Don't say a word until I tell you." Pause.

The Israelites marched a second time around the walls of Jericho. The people kept perfectly quiet. Pause. **The trumpets sounded as the people marched.** Pause. **Still the walls stood firm.** Pause.

The people in Jericho were still afraid. Pause.

Joshua reminded his people not to say a word. Pause.

The people continued marching three, four, five, six times around the city. Pause. **The trumpets sounded as the people marched.** Pause. **Still the walls stood firm.** Pause.

The people in Jericho were still afraid. Pause.

During the seventh time around, Joshua commanded, "The Lord has given you this city. This time, when the trumpets sound, you can shout! When you get into the city, spare Rahab and her family."

As soon as the trumpets sounded again (pause), **the people let out a mighty shout!** Pause. **The walls of Jericho fell with a loud crash.** Pause.

God helped the Israelites defeat Jericho. Joshua remembered how Rahab had helped and encouraged the spies. So he sent the

two spies to get Rahab, her father, mother, brothers, and all those with her and take them to a safe place outside the city. Rahab and her family then lived with the Israelites.

> ### TEACHER TIP
> If you have time, switch sound effects roles. If you do this, have a bowl of soapy water and a towel close by so you can wash the *trumpets* before other kids use them.

After the skit, put the *trumpets* away, and have the children give themselves a standing ovation for their outstanding performances. Have them remain standing, then say: **Raise your hand when you've thought of an answer to each of the questions I'm about to ask you. I'd like to hear lots of different, interesting answers. When someone gives an answer you've thought of and you don't have anything more to add, you may sit down. When everyone is seated, I'll ask you all to stand again for the next question.** Ask:

- **Why do you think the Israelites wanted to follow Joshua?** (Because he followed God; they trusted him; he was their leader.)
- **How do you think the Israelite army felt when the walls of Jericho came tumbling down? Explain.** (Good, because God was faithful; surprised, because they didn't know what God would do; a little scared, because they had never seen anything like that happen before.)
- **How do you think Rahab felt knowing she had helped the Israelites?** (Glad she had helped them; happy her family was safe; thankful she had made the right decision.)
- **What do you think makes Joshua a hero?** (He trusted God; he led the people in the right way; he listened to God.)

the POINT

Say: **True heroes encourage others to follow God. That's what made Joshua a hero!** Ask:

- **What heroes do you know who are like Joshua?** (None; my parents; my pastor.)

Say: **Joshua encouraged others to trust that God would help them knock down Jericho's walls. Let's learn more about encouraging others to follow God.**

SUPERHEROES
(up to 13 minutes)

Give each person a pencil and a photocopy of the "Hold Up the Light" handout (p. 168). Form groups of three and assign each group one of these passages: **Matthew 5:14-16; Titus 2:7-8;** or **James 3:17-18.** It's OK if more than one group has the same Bible passage.

> ### TEACHER TIP
> If groups have trouble getting started, offer these ideas:
>
> - **Matthew 5:14-16**—"Do good things" or "Live a good life."
> - **Titus 2:7-8**—"Be an example and do good" or "Speak the truth."
> - **James 3:17-18**—"Help people who are troubled" or "Be peaceful."

Say: **On your handout, put a check mark next to the Bible passage I assigned to your group. Read your passage aloud together, then discuss what it says about how we can encourage others to follow God. Write your group's message in the space on your handout. Then, inside the light bulb, write or draw one way you can "light the way" and encourage someone to follow God this week. For example, you might write, "I'll bring my friend to church next Sunday." Sign your initials on the superhero's chest as a symbol of your commitment.**

While kids are working, tape a sheet of newsprint to a wall. Write

"Ways to encourage others to follow God" on the newsprint.

After four minutes, blow the *trumpet* twice, and wait for kids to respond. Gather kids in front of the newsprint. Have volunteers from each group read their passages. Have other volunteers share their groups' ideas about what the passages say about encouraging others. Then have volunteers share how they'll encourage someone to follow God this week. Write all the ideas on the newsprint with markers. Ask:

● **Why does God want us to encourage others to follow him?** (So they can know God; because the Bible says so; because God loves everyone.)

● **How have people encouraged you to follow God?** (By teaching me about Jesus; by taking me to church; by praying for me; by telling me about the Bible.)

● **How do you feel about encouraging someone to follow God? Explain.** (Good, because I know I'm pleasing God; nervous, because I might mess up.)

the POINT

Say: **True heroes encourage others to follow God. You've each come up with some great ways to be a true hero this week by encouraging someone to follow Christ! Now let's have our own awards ceremony for the true heroes we have in our class.**

Hands-On FUN AT HOME

We believe that Christian education extends beyond the classroom into the home. Photocopy the "Hands-On Fun at Home" handout (p. 169) for this week, and send it home with your kids. Encourage kids to try several activities and discuss the Bible verses and questions with their parents.

CLOSING

LEARNING LAB

HERO AWARDS
(up to 13 minutes)

Have kids gather by the *Celluclay* shapes from the last lesson. Say: **Last week we made these shapes to help us remember how God loves and cares for us. Now that the shapes are dry, we can use markers to decorate them as medallions. When you're finished, I'll cut a piece of string for you to thread through your shape. Tie the ends of the string together, and make a medallion necklace like award-winning people receive.**

Supply colorful markers, and have kids decorate their shapes. Have construction paper and markers available for kids who didn't make clay shapes last week. Let those kids each draw a medallion on their paper, decorate it, and cut it out.

When kids finish, supply different lengths of *neon kite string* (if you have enough left) or colorful yarn. Help children thread the string through the hole in the shapes and tie the two ends of the string together.

Say: **In a few moments, we're going to hold an awards ceremony for all the heroes in this classroom. But first, form pairs for this activity.**

Have partners stand next to each other in a circle. Then say: **And now for our awards ceremony. One at a time, affirm your partner by saying, "**(Your partner's name) **encourages others to follow God. What a hero!" Then put your partner's medallion around his or her neck. Then your partner will do the same for you. We'll go around the circle until everyone has received a hero award.**

Play the "Hero Award" segment of the *cassette tape* while kids present their awards.

After everyone has accepted a medallion, say: **True heroes encourage others to follow God. True heroes stand up for what they believe, trust in God, and follow God's directions. Isn't it neat to be in a room full of friends who are true heroes?**

the POINT

Have kids join hands in the circle. Pray: **Dear God, as we wear our medallions home, help us encourage others to follow you. We thank you for loving us and caring for us every day. In Jesus' name, amen.**

HOLD UP the LIGHT

"You are the light that gives light to the world" (Matthew 5:14a).

- Place a check mark in the box next to the passage you've been assigned.

  ❑ Matthew 5:14-16 ❑ Titus 2:7-8 ❑ James 3:17-18

- Read your passage together.
- What does your passage say about how you can encourage others to follow God? Write your ideas below:

- Now, think of one way you can be a light for Christ and encourage others to follow him. Write or draw your idea in the light bulb.
- Write your initials on one hero's chest as a commitment that you'll pursue your idea this week!

LESSON 13:
SHOW THEM THE WAY

the POINT True heroes encourage others to follow God.

BIBLE FOCUS

"Be strong and brave. Don't be afraid, because the Lord your God will be everywhere you go" (Joshua 1:9).

FAITH walk

Each night this week before bedtime, set aside 10 to 15 minutes for family Bible-reading time. Read about different Bible heroes who encouraged others to follow God. For example, read about John the Baptist (Matthew 3), the crippled man (Acts 3:1-10), Philip (Acts 8:26-40), Lydia (Acts 16:13-15), Apollos (Acts 18:24-28), Timothy (Philippians 2:19-22), and Paul (Acts 9:1-19). Talk about how these heroes led so many people to God. Thank God for these super, extraordinary Bible heroes, and ask God to help your family learn from their examples.

LAUGH it UP

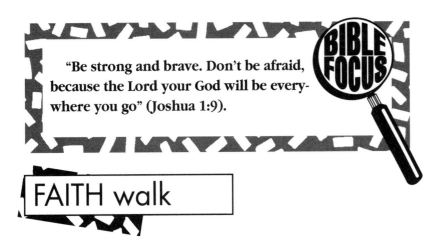

MARC HAD AN INTERESTING WAY OF BRINGING PEOPLE TO CHURCH.

Hands-On FUN AT HOME

CHECK it OUT

Read 1 John 3:7.
How can you tell the difference between someone who wants to lead you *to* God and someone who wants to lead you *away* from God?

Read Proverbs 10:17.
How does "accepting correction" lead us toward God?

Read 1 Corinthians 11:1.
How can you be an example of Christ?

WAY to PRAY

Give each family member a pencil and a sheet of paper. Have family members each think of a friend who doesn't follow God. Ask them to write four ways they can encourage these friends to follow God, such as inviting them to church or Sunday school or telling them about God's love. Say, "Each day this week, pray for your friend. Then use one of your suggestions to introduce the person to your true friend, Jesus."

BONUS IDEAS

GREAT GAMES

True Hero-Tack-Toe—Use four *terry ropes* to form a Tick-Tack-Toe game board on the floor. Use *prism shapes* with the shiny side up for one player and *prism shapes* with the shiny side down for the other. Before a player places a piece, he or she must name a Bible hero and one thing the hero did.

Form more game boards by using pieces of *neon kite string* or colorful yarn. Use *paper balls* for game pieces.

This game works well with the lessons on Joshua.

Egypt-Canaan-Mountains-Desert—Play this game in a large open space. Write each of these locations on separate sheets of poster board: "Egypt," "Canaan," "mountains," "desert." Tape one sheet of poster board to each of the four walls of the room. Gather kids on the Canaan side of the room. Say: **I'll call out different locations for you to travel to. See if you can be the first one to reach the location. Ready? Mountains!**

Randomly call out locations. Try these ideas during the game:

- Vary the way kids can travel by saying, "Hop to the desert" or "Take giant steps to the mountains."
- As you call out one location, point in the opposite direction.
- Tell kids that any time you say "Pharaoh," they must stand with their legs apart and their hands above their heads to form a pyramid shape.

This game works well with the lessons on Joseph and on the Ten Commandments.

Grab the Grain—Play this game in a large open space. Form two equal teams, and have them line up on opposite sides of the room. Place the *paper balls* in the center of the room. Have the kids number off as shown (see diagram).

Say: **You are Israelites who try to get grain and bring it home from Egypt. The *paper balls* are the grain. I'll call out a number. The two kids who have that number will hop to the center, pick up**

a *paper ball,* hop back to their sides, touch the wall, and yell, "I'm home!" The first person who yells gets to keep the *paper ball.* The other person will put the *paper ball* back in the center. Be careful not to bump heads as you pick up the *paper balls.* The second pair of racers will take baby steps to the center, the third pair will take giant steps, and the fourth pair will skip to the center. We'll continue until I call all the numbers or until all the *paper balls* are gone from the center. Then we'll count each team's *paper balls.* The team with the most *paper balls* will be awarded the trophy from the Learning Lab.

Call a number and start the game. Caution kids to be careful not to fall or bump heads. Make sure everyone has a chance to race at least once. Encourage all team members to shout encouraging words and cheers for their teammates. Declare a winner, and let the winning team members hold the trophy over their heads and give themselves a cheer. Then have everyone give high fives.

This game works well with the lessons on Joseph.

AFFIRMATION ACTIVITIES

Pass a Compliment—Sit with kids in a circle. Bring out two differently colored *paper balls.* Pass one ball to the person on your left, and say something about that person that makes him or her a true hero. Pass the other colored ball to the person on your right, and say something good about that person. For example, you could say, "You're a hero because you're friendly to everyone" or "You're a hero because your sense of humor makes others feel good." Each time a person passes a ball, he or she compliments the next person in the circle. At some point the two *paper balls* will cross, and one person will say something nice to two people.

After one round, have kids, find a new position in the circle. Play again, having kids affirm new people. Vary the game by adding more *paper balls* to the circle.

This game works well with Lesson 13.

Commandment Award—After the lessons on the Ten Commandments, award the *miniature trophy* to kids who have done something outstanding to honor their parents, to treat their families right, or to please God.

Each week, have kids each write on an index card their names and what they did to follow one of the commandments. Place all the index cards in a container. Mix them up, then draw one out. Read the card, and have that person step to the front of the classroom and receive the *miniature trophy.* Have everyone give the person a rousing round of applause.

Take an instant-print photograph of the trophy winner. Tack the photograph to a bulletin board titled "Commandment Award-Winners."

The following week, repeat the process by having kids who haven't won fill out cards with their commandment accomplishments. Continue until your bulletin board is full of photographs. Make sure each student has a picture on the board.

Just for You—Write the following affirmations on a sheet of newsprint, and tape the newsprint to a wall.

- I'm a fan of yours because...
- This trophy is an award for being the best...because...
- If I could give you a gift, it would be...because...

Have kids sit in a circle. Place the *straw fan, miniature trophy,* and *gift box* in the center. Say: **I'll begin an affirmation time in which we'll say good things about each other. I'll choose one of the Learning Lab items in the center, give it to the person on my right, and complete one of the phrases from the newsprint. For example, I could take the *straw fan,* give it to** (name), **and say, "I'm a fan of yours because you always help when it's time to clean up." Then** (name) **will put the fan back, choose another item from the center, give it to the person on his** (or her) **right, and complete one of the phrases from the newsprint. Each person in the circle has to be affirmed before anyone else can receive a second compliment.**

Continue until everyone has been affirmed. Then offer a prayer thanking God for each person in the circle. (Be sure to say each person's name when you pray.)

An "Arm Load" of Compliments—Give each student a marker and a pad of self-stick notes. (Or give each person slips of paper and tape.) Each person will need one note for each student in the class.

Say: **When I blow the *trumpet* once, write a compliment on a self-stick note, then stick it on a person's arm. Do this for each person in our class. You could write things like "fun," "kind," "patient," "tells great jokes," or "friendly." By the end of the affirmation time, each person will have an "arm load" of compliments to read and take home.**

Blow the *trumpet* once and let the affirmation time begin. After everyone is finished, blow the *trumpet* again, and have everyone sit in a circle. Encourage kids to read their affirmation notes and take them home to post in their rooms.

PARTIES AND PROJECTS

Treat-Your-Family Party—Have your class plan a party for parents and siblings. (Encourage kids who have no brothers or sisters to invite friends or younger students from other classes.)

Supply treats such as ice cream, cookies, and toppings. Let kids fix sundaes for their families as an example of how to treat their families right.

Give each family a sheet of paper and a pencil. Have families work together to write a recipe for treating each other right. Here's an example:

Treat-Each-Other-Right Treats

1 cup of kisses
1½ cups of hugs
1 pound of forgiveness
½ cup of "I love yous"
kindness—to taste

This party works well with the lessons on Joseph.

Camp-In—Host an indoor camping party when the weather is too wet to camp outside. Set up a campground in your classroom, a gym, or a fellowship hall. Have kids bring tents, lawn chairs, sleeping bags, and flashlights. Go outside and gather stones. Bring them inside, and arrange them in a circle to represent a fire pit.

Try these activities:

- **Horseshoes**—Use two empty 2-liter soft drink containers weighted with sand or stones for posts, and use cardboard rings for horseshoes.
- **Crab Kickball**—Form two teams to play a game of kickball. Have everyone play the game in a "crab" position—walking on hands and feet, facing up.
- **Wild Hike**—Hand out flashlights, turn off the lights, and lead everyone on a hike through the dark church.
- **Campfire Food**—Serve hot dogs, soft drinks, chips, and S'mores (a graham cracker, marshmallow, and chocolate sandwich toasted, broiled, or microwaved without its top until the marshmallow turns light brown).
- **Campfire Songs**—Close by turning off the lights, turning on a few flashlights, and singing favorite songs.

Coffee Break Cookies—Volunteer to have your students serve cookies, coffee, and juice following a church service. Plan a Saturday baking party. Have kids bring ingredients, and work together to bake cookies. Or you could have kids bake cookies at home and bring them to church the day you serve. While cookies are baking or while groups are arranging cookies, read the story of Jesus washing his disciples' feet **(John 13:1-20).** Discuss what it means to serve and how it feels to serve. When the time comes, have the kids serve the cookies with a smile!

Human Scroll—With your students, make a mural of the story of Joseph for kids in a younger class. Staple together several sheets of newsprint to make a huge scroll. Have kids write a title for their story and the reference **(Genesis 37–45)** at the beginning of their scroll. Then have them draw pictures of Joseph's story—receiving the coat of many colors, being sold by his jealous brothers, being in prison, serving as food distributor, and making up with his brothers, for example. Practice rolling the newsprint around one child to make a human scroll. Make sure the paper is loose enough so the child can walk.

The next week, plan with the younger children's teacher to have your class lead the younger group. Bring along some snacks to share. Sing songs and play games. Then have younger children help unroll the human scroll and tell Joseph's story from the pictures. At the end of the story, roll up the scroll without the child in it, and give it to the younger children.

Good-Thoughts Project—Talk about how true heroes are people of action. Then have kids brainstorm projects to encourage others—projects that would please God. For example, they might suggest collecting canned goods for a food pantry, making and delivering cards to residents of nursing homes, or going on a litter hunt in a nearby park.

Write all the ideas on a sheet of newsprint. Have kids vote on one idea for the class to do. Then do it! Have kids create posters announcing the project and inviting the congregation to participate. Then have your class gather and deliver the items or head the work teams.